# CONDITIONI SWIMMERS

## A GUIDE TO LAND-BASED TRAINING

# Alan Lynn
## Foreword by Cecil Colwin

THE CROWOOD PRESS

First published in 2007 by
The Crowood Press Ltd
Ramsbury, Marlborough
Wiltshire SN8 2HR

www.crowood.com

**British Library Cataloguing-in-Publication Data**
A catalogue record for this book is available from the British Library.

ISBN 978 1 86126 913 3

**Disclaimer**
Please note that the author and the publisher of this book do not accept any
responsibility whatsoever for any error or omission, nor any loss, injury, damage,
adverse outcome or liability suffered as a result of the use of the information contained
in this book, or reliance upon it. Since conditioning exercises can be dangerous and
could involve physical activities that are too strenuous for some individuals to engage in
safely, it is essential that a doctor be consulted before undertaking training.

**Dedication**
This book is dedicated to my wife Jacqueline and son Cameron, with love and thanks for
their support and patience, and also to my mum, Anna, without whom this fantastic
swimming journey would not have started.

Typeset and designed by Outhouse!
Shalbourne, Marlborough, Wiltshire SN8 3QJ

Printed and bound in Spain by Graphy Cems

# Contents

# Acknowledgements

The author and publishers would like to thank the following for their help in the production of this book: Bradley Hay, who patiently demonstrated most of the exercises for the photographs; the swimmers from Stirling ASC and Stirling Swimming for appearing in the other pictures; and to the National Swimming Academy at Stirling University for the use of their excellent facilities. Thanks also to British Swimming for granting permission to reproduce figs 12, 14 and 15.

Special thanks to Scottish Institute of Sport (SIS) swimming coaches Chris Martin and Ciaran O'Brien for their suggestions and comments on the various drafts of the book, and also to SIS Strength and Conditioning coaches Dave Clark and Jamie Youngson for their input to the book and continued efforts to help Scottish swimmers go faster.

# Foreword

*Conditioning for Swimmers* is a rare and insightful book that leaves no doubt as to the dramatic improvement to be derived from a regimen of intelligently applied land training. A commendable work, based on much study as well as successful practical experience, this book will enthuse and motivate coaches and swimmers alike. What impressed me most is the thought and explanation given to every conceivable phase of modern land-training for swimmers at all levels of development.

The author's knowledge and skill as a successful international coach and conditioner stems from much practical experience as well as from his work as an educator who has diligently researched and studied the history, scientific pros and cons, and philosophical aspects of his subject. The text illustrates each exercise and how it fits into British Swimming's Long Term Athlete Development (LTAD) plan, together with periodized training programmes for all five LTAD levels, as first conceived by Bill Sweetenham, British Swimming's National Performance Director.

Discussed in depth are the benefits of various types of training, together with an analysis of the types of equipment involved. The book deals lucidly and at length with how to apply a cyclic step-by-step programme of progressive overload vital to the success of the modern competitive swimmer. The unique text provides detailed exercise prescriptions, training plans and charts for swimmers from age-group to the elite; warming-up, stretch-

ing, safety precautions, general as well as stroke-specific routines, weight-training, medicine ball, and Swiss ball exercises, stretchcord resistance-training exercises – you name it. This book is a winner!

*Cecil Colwin, 2007*

'Thanks to Alan for putting together an unparalleled modern compendium of dryland methods and equipment.'
*Murray Stephens*
*Chief Executive Officer, North Baltimore Aquatic Club (NBAC)*

# CHAPTER 1

# Background

Training techniques and coaching practice in the sport of competitive swimming have evolved significantly in the past thirty years. New ideas and concepts like training prescribed from blood lactate testing have come and gone amid great controversy in the coaching fraternity. Sleek new 'high-tech' equipment, such as 'Fastskin' racing suits, have literally changed the visual spectacle of the sport and, despite valiant efforts by key individuals (Forbes Carlile, Cecil Colwin and John Leonard in particular), the spectre of chemically enhanced performances still casts a dark cloud over certain aspects of the sport.

However, there are some constants in swimming, the only sport where humans actually propel themselves through a 'foreign' environment without the aid of propulsive devices. The structure of age-group swimming, a much-maligned area of the sport, is pretty much the same now as it was in the early 1970s. Children learn to swim, they join swimming clubs and, through a progressive series of squads, they improve their performances. Despite a more professional structure in the sport, much of the infrastructure in swimming across the world still relies on the work of dedicated volunteers each week, staffing meets, running clubs and serving on committees. Another constant, perhaps surprising given the technical advancements in all sports in recent years, is the practice of land training, i.e. conditioning work done outside of the pool itself. As will be demonstrated and discussed in this book, despite much change in other areas of swimming, 'dryland', to use the North American vernacular, has not changed much in the thirty-odd years since Mark Spitz won seven gold medals in Munich 1972. There have been some developments in training procedures – for example, the programming and scheduling of training commonly known as periodization – but the basic exercises, equipment and training sessions are not remarkably different from those completed by the forebears of today's aquatic superstars like Michael Phelps, Laure Manadou, Ian Thorpe and Leisl Jones.

This may seem to be a remarkable claim, but it is borne out by the facts of the author's own coaching experience and research, and by the published information in refereed and sport-specific journals. It is not, as may be misinterpreted by some readers, intended to be a criticism of coaching practice, merely the statement of a reality already known through anecdotal sources and experience. There is a school of thought in sport that goes something like 'if it ain't broke, don't fix it', and there is an element of this kind of thinking prevalent in land-training practice. If anything has changed recently, it is perhaps a stronger emphasis on 'strength training' using free weights in particular. This is not a development supported by all coaches and, as will be debated and outlined in other sections of this book, not entirely favoured by the author either.

From the early days of 'coaching' in swimming there have been innovators and artisans who dared to be different in their methods. People like Americans Bob Kiphuth and Ernst Vornbrock, physical educators by day and swimming coaches by night. These men applied scientific principles from many fields to their coaching practice in an attempt to produce better performances. All of them had a belief that conditioning outside of the pool could, and would, positively influence performance in competition. This underpinning philosophy still exists and, despite little in the way of supportive empirical evidence (then or now), land-based training in its many forms remains a fixture in the overall preparation programmes of swimming coaches today. This of course does not mean that land training does not work, only that scientists have not yet proved what most coaches already know – it does!

So what is different about land training from the 1960s and 70s and that performed today, if anything? Certainly the equipment is shinier, the colours brighter and the facilities more modern, but the actual practices and routines of the swimmers and coaches are not so different. A glance at swimming coaching texts in the past four decades shows little attention being paid to land training other than photographs of swimmers stretching or occasionally performing some conditioning exercises on fixed resistance machines. There is very little information about the range of land-training options available in designing programmes and almost nothing about how to effectively integrate land and pool-based training for maximum effectiveness. Some notable exceptions to this are books by coaches Buck Dawson and John Hogg, which although they are more than thirty years old, still hold true to the basic tenets of this book – that land training if done properly can and will improve swimming performance. Dawson's book (*The Complete Book of Dry-Land Exercises for Swimming*, 1964) in particular is a gem because it outlines different forms of training (strength, stamina and suppleness), highlights good practice from élite coaches across the world (Counsilman, Talbot, Kiphuth, etc.) and above all sends the message that land training is an essential component of effective swimming training.

There are a few books that purport to be about land training for swimming (astute readers will know which books I mean), but they are just regurgitated strength and conditioning theories with a couple of pages linking them to swimming. These have been misleading swimming coaches for years about the real value of land-based training. In fact, they may have led to injuries, misdirected training programmes and, in some extreme cases, retirement from the sport. Coaches who have relied on such books need search no further!

Another admirable exception to this generic, 'get stronger and swim faster approach' is the legendary work of James 'Doc' Counsilman. In all of his books, from the earliest *The Science of Swimming* text in 1968, he places a high value on the use of land training, including some discussion on the integration of land and pool training, which very few others have managed to do since. Of course 'Doc' was instrumental in devising several land-training tools still in use today, most notably the 'swimbench', which is discussed in the training section of this book. Throughout his coaching career, Counsilman was a strong advocate for the use of land training, a legacy that still lives on beyond his sad passing in 2004.

More recently, and with the assistance of modern technology, British experts Bob Smith and Henryk Lakomy have produced a CD-rom with video clips of strength and

*Fig. 1. Age-group swimmers participating in land training.*

conditioning exercises for swimming, which is another excellent addition to the field.

## LAND TRAINING: WHAT IS IT?

Land training for swimming (dryland as described previously) refers to any activity done out of the water designed to improve performance in the water in some way. There are many benefits in land training for swimming and there are also many different activities included under the land-training banner. Methods included are: stretching, medicine ball work, Swiss ball activities, circuit training, stretchcords, running, weights, swimbenches and, occasionally, participating in other sports. Land training is essentially cross-training performed out of the pool. In fact the sport of triathlon was created from the needs of (track)

athletes to vary their training stimulus with 'cross-training' in the pool and on bikes.

Before puberty, a common goal of land training is to improve general athleticism. At all age groups, land training is used to improve balance, proprioception and body awareness, strength, mobility and flexibility. To achieve a high level of performance in swimming the performer needs to have good core strength, i.e. in the hips, abdomen and lower back, as swimmers can generate power from the hips and land training is an excellent means of developing this. The better the athlete you are, the better your potential as a swimmer, and land training gives extra balance and added value to the pool-based swimming programme. There are many issues to be aware of for the coach when designing the land-training programme. As in the pool, technique in the performance of the

*Fig. 2. Core-stability training.*

land-training activity is the key to success and obtaining maximum benefits. The dryland programme should also be designed for stroke/distance specificity, and the annual, periodized training plan should reflect this.

Core-stability work (involving the hips, abdomen and lower back working together in flexion/extension, lateral flexion and rotation with flexion and extension) is a good land-training activity. The function of the 'core' is to align the posture dynamically, which will allow elongation to get the streamline effect that is needed for efficiency in the water, and to act as a force couple between the arms and legs. Abdominal strength is essential to fast swimming as strong abdominals allow the swimmer to control body position, leading to more efficient swimming; it also helps to contribute to faster starts and turns. As illustrated in Fig. 2, a 'physio' or 'Swiss' ball is an excellent tool for doing core work. A full explanation of core-stability training and exercises is provided in Chapter 3.

Medicine-ball training is another excellent dryland method for swimmers as it is safe, easy to use, versatile and adaptable. The two main things to work on are rotations/twists and throws, as these utilize and work the core, arms and shoulders. Medicine-ball

*Fig. 3. Medicine-ball training.*

*Fig. 4. A swimmer training with dumb-bells.*

their team spirit and improves body awareness and co-ordination. The benefits of fast-paced aerobic games include improved co-ordination, and general athleticism, which benefit the swimmer because the better an athlete you are, the better you will turn, start and be able to change your stroke because of increased body awareness. Examples of games include tunnel tig, battleships and so on. Many coaches take the view that these activities help build these qualities in young swimmers and that the fun and motivation that these activities hold for the young swimmers will keep more of them in the sport for longer. The specific issue of land training for younger swimmers is discussed in Chapter 4.

Mistakenly, many coaches and swimmers see land training as being only about weight or resistance training, when this is only a small component of a well-balanced dryland training programme. When lifting weights, the coach must make the actions swim-specific utilizing all the stabilizing muscles. Machine-weights systems are not as good as free weights, as they eliminate the use of 'stabilizers' and generally work only in one plane of movement; thus for swimming, dumb-bells would be a preferable form of weight training. Some coaches advocate that weight training is needed only after the athlete has done a lot of progression through bodyweight exercises first and that resistance exercises used for swimming should be multi-joint exercises or arranged in a circuit style to benefit the swimmer the most. The reasoning behind this is related to sport-specificity, as swimming involves the whole body. This book is not specifically about weight training and as such does not include details of many traditional resistance exercises, but some information is provided about the key exercises required and, more significantly, the planning of strength training within an overall land- and pool-based training plan.

training is recommended to a swimmer because of the similarity of speed of movement between the two activities. Categorized as plyometric training, this is the swimming equivalent of the jumps and bounds used by land-based athletes to improve their power. Details of medicine ball exercises and plyometric training are also shown in Chapter 3.

For young swimmers, fast-paced aerobic games and circuits are a good extra aerobic workout, which keeps them motivated, builds

*Fig. 5. A swimmer using a stretchcord.*

Surgical tubing or stretchcords are an excellent and beneficial form of dryland training. These cords allow the athlete to have a constant resistance throughout a sport-specific movement. Stretchcord training can be done with time as a guide for repetitions or early in the development stages using fatigue as a guide. Stretchcord exercises include strengthening the internal and external shoulder rotators to prevent shoulder injury, teaching and strengthening the catch phase of the stroke, and all other phases of all strokes, movements and kicks in swimming. A more advanced form of this training is the swimbench (if one is available). A swimbench can be a strength trainer or an aerobic exerciser, depending on the way it is used. A swimbench can also allow the coach to help teach technique in any of the four swim strokes, and eliminate bad technique, which can lead to injury or poor results. Details of stretchcord and swimbench exercises and training programmes are provided in Chapter 3.

Flexibility or range of movement (ROM) is the ability to achieve optimal positions in the water for the application of force and the minimization of drag. Efficiency of movement requires the appropriate amount of joint motion. Stretching is a good way of obtaining flexibility with less flexible areas worked on more rather than a whole-body approach. There are different types of stretching including static, proprioceptive neuromuscular facilitation (PNF) and dynamic. Flexibility is usually worked on outside of the water and is therefore a legitimate dryland-training technique. Stretching a muscle causes the fibres in the muscle to lengthen; longer muscle fibres generate more contraction force than shorter fibres, which are caused by the build-up of lactic acid. Stretching also increases range of motion, which has the following benefits for a

11

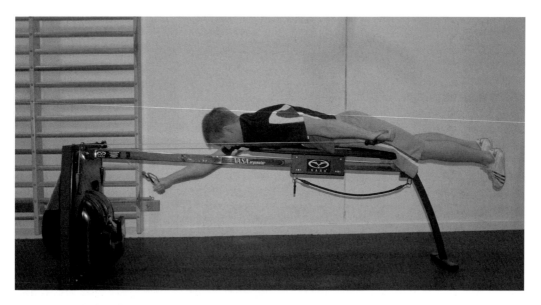

*Fig. 6. A swimbench.*

breaststroker: increases the safety of the kicking movement; increases the distance the foot travels in each propulsive movement; and keeps the foot more effectively oriented throughout the kicking movement. For all strokes, an increase in the range of motion around the shoulder will lead to increased stroke length and less energy expended in performing the movement. Although extremely well covered in other more specific books, some information and illustrations on stretching as part of the recovery process are provided in Chapter 3.

In summary, dryland training is an important part of a swimmer's training routine. Not only does it fine-tune the élite athlete but it can also motivate junior athletes and keep them in the sport. The combination of dryland training techniques used by a coach will always remain one of personal preference, but the intensity and technique with which the activities are done will ultimately determine the success or otherwise of the programme.

This book dares to be different in that it sets out the details of the key land-training methods employed in successful swimming programmes and it attempts to outline how to incorporate these techniques and methods in successful training and preparation programmes for swimmers of all ages and abilities. It is not simply another 'how to lift weights, get stronger and hope this means you swim faster' book. What follows is a very short exploration of the key issues and debates around the value of land training for competitive swimming.

## Land Training: Some Thoughts on the 'Value' Debate

The following comment appeared on the 'Supertraining' listserv a few years ago, made by the forum moderator, Dr Mel Siff:

Similarly, 'functional training' with specific supplementary drills enhances skills with those drills and not necessarily those of the sport itself. We ought not to forget that so-called 'functional training' happens to be rather mythical in nature and that sport specific training does not rely primarily on the use of exercises, which appear to be very similar to one's sporting movements. Instead, 'functional training' ('sport specific training') needs to enhance the motor qualities (such as maximum strength, speed-strength and speed-endurance) and rely far more on special sports skill training to integrate those qualities into each relevant sport.

'Functional training' then has become a bit of a loose term that commonly finds its way into the everyday language of coaches, physiotherapists and strength coaches. The basic idea is that exercises should mimic sport activities as closely as possible in order to enhance or transfer to sport performance. While I am oversimplifying the actual meaning of 'functional training', I would like to discuss more fully the idea of specificity because the two concepts are related. The statement by Siff (above) was made in the context of using mirrors and other devices and methods as simultaneous feedback for the development of sport skills, much in the way that dancers have used mirrors for decades. The studies being discussed in this context showed mixed results, but a number of studies showed that, at least with novice learners, the use of such simultaneous feedback was detrimental to learning and that using drills that too closely mimicked the sport skill actually resulted in reduced performance later on. This kind of problem is well known in motor learning and control circles and is called 'negative transfer'.

A common example of negative transfer is what happens in the near-simultaneous instruction of both water skiing and snow skiing, or in badminton and tennis. Practising one skill actually impedes the learning of a subsequent skill because the techniques are too similar, resulting in interference of learning. The concept of sport-specificity is one of the most powerful, profound and far-reaching concepts in all of athlete training. Sadly, specificity is also one of the most misunderstood concepts. According to the tenets of specificity, the best way to train for a sport is simply to do the sport itself. Obviously there is no more specific performance of a sport skill than the skill itself. However, we know that this idea does not result in optimal or maximal performance. Often the athlete is simply too weak, stiff or lacks the stamina to perform the skill techniques adequately, and by 'trying' to perform the finished skill without the requisite strength, power, flexibility, etc., the athlete develops bad habits that plague the athlete for the rest of his/her performances of that skill. Think of the age-group swimmer who lacks the necessary strength to swim butterfly and subsequently develops a very poor technique, which is difficult to change in later years. Moreover, in events such as running we know that a 1,500m athlete should not simply go out and run a mile everyday at race-pace. The athlete's performance on subsequent race-pace miles will deteriorate rapidly after the first attempt and further performance enhancement declines rapidly. This is why such methods as 'interval training' evolved. Coaches found that performing shorter distances at similar and faster times allowed the athlete to perform more total work, and the greater total work was responsible for improved performances.

Marathon runners are good examples of athletes who use non-specific training. How successful would a marathoner be if he/she ran 26.2 miles in every training session? By analogy in swimming, in order to follow the specificity principle to its logical conclusion, we should simply have swimmers race their best stroke and distance every session. Obviously,

*Fig. 7. Weight training.*

this simply does not work. Swimming requires careful, thorough and consistent training in all the aspects of performance technique in order to achieve élite performance. The principle of progression intrudes on the principle of specificity. A balance between progression and specificity must be achieved. So where does this leave us? Should we train specifically? The answer is yes, but not exclusively.

A valid and confirmatory source of evidence in support of land-based training is the fact that the vast majority of swimmers across the world actually perform land training as part of their weekly routine; therefore by implication it contributes something to performance. My own research shows that most coaches take the pragmatic view that land training contributes more to sprints than distance events and to the more power-based strokes such as butterfly and breaststroke. However, this is not enough to conclude anything of substance about its value. There is considerable debate (and at times controversy) about whether or not land training contributes anything at all to performance.

Objective quantification of performance contributions may give statisticians numbers to manipulate (although there are not many numbers to compute in this debate), but the opinions of the world's leading swimming scientists are also relevant. Australian sports scientist (Professor) Brent Rushall, who has worked with élite swimmers and coaches across the world for more than forty years, states (1998, p. 4):

> Weights and out-of-water work do not enhance performance. Weights and cross training are performed in the belief that specific physical benefits will be produced and in

turn those benefits will be incorporated into swimming techniques. Muscles trained in isolation do not transfer benefits to whole-body activities such as swimming. Specific exercise improvements cannot be 're-educated' into complex swimming strokes.

Exercising with weights or other land activities promotes fitness and improvements that cannot be used in swimming. If they are followed at the expense of pool time or inhibit recovery from beneficial pool experiences, they are detrimental practices. High frequency and high resistance weight exercises are a common cause of swimming injury.

There is probably a place for weight and cross-training in swimming. Land work is only valuable in the early stages of physical capacity training and should be completed prior to the commencement of specific technique training. Resistance training and exercising should occur no more than once a week in an élite program and preferably, it should only employ exercises that use the whole body at a time (e.g. medicine ball work and gymnastics).

This view concedes that land training probably does assist with general preparation, as long as it is integrated properly into the programme, but it does not categorically support the views and common practice of most coaches: that land training can and does improve performance. The actual training programmes of most élite swimmers around the world would be in complete contrast to this position with somewhere between three and six dryland sessions per week the norm throughout most of the season (tapering is a different matter and will be discussed later). The position taken by Rushall also makes the classic, and mistaken, assumption that effective land training is largely about weight training. The author actually agrees with the contention that weights alone do not improve performance, but there is so much more to land training than this.

Another leading swimming scientist is US physiologist (Professor) David Costill, who states (1998, p. 1):

Swimming strength is important. Upper body strength is a good predictor of success. If sprint swimming were correlated to power the coefficients would be significant. Sprinters can be differentiated from distance swimmers by the power they can generate.

This looks promising, but he also concludes (Costill, 1998, p. 2):

Supplementary land training provides no added benefit. The lack of specificity in the land training is a drawback. You can gain strength by swimming. If you want to overload the muscles then do sprint swimming.

Once again the academics fail to recognize that although they cannot prove why, the practices of coaches and swimmers do not support the hypothesis that land training does not work. Improving performance is such a complex affair, that isolating any small part of the picture and drawing conclusions from it is a dangerous practice. Maybe in a controlled study there is no significant statistical relationship between an isolated strength measure and sprinting performance, but did the swimmers in the Costill investigation swim faster in the meet they tapered for that season? Swimming coaches are generally fairly sceptical about sports scientists anyway and when they read such statements compared to what they actually do, they become further inured and ignore what might be (potentially) worthwhile information.

It is back to the practitioners again to make the case for land-training contributions to performance. British coach Clive Rushton, in a coach education review for New Zealand's *Swimming*, summarizes (2003, p. 3):

Land training for swimming is seen as a vital contributor to our success yet is totally misunderstood by most swimming coaches and other conditioning specialists.

There is no 'meeting of minds' on this at all. The coaches and experts that I interviewed in the course of my research were all in agreement with the 'practitioner' side of this debate, but no clear consensus on the precise contributions of land training to swimming performance was reached. What is clear is that coaches and swimmers believe that land training has a worthwhile contribution to make and that no one has yet 'proved' what that contribution might be.

Not a controlled study, but valid evidence of the relationship of land training to race distances nonetheless, is an investigation study done by Genadijus Sokolovas at the 2000 US Olympic trials. He found that:

1. Sprinters and distance swimmers have similar average weekly land-training hours and number of sessions per week, but distance swimmers have significantly higher weekly swimming workload volume and number of hours spent swimming than sprinters. This means that distance swimmers swim higher volume workouts than sprinters, as would be expected.
2. Male and female trials qualifiers had similar swimming and land-training workload volume. There were no significant differences in training-load parameters between females and males, but male freestyle sprinters have significantly higher land-training workload volume than female freestyle sprinters.
3. Female sprinters, as well as male sprinters, and distance swimmers have a tendency to increase land-training workload volume with age, but it does not seem to have an influence on performance progression, since there is a negative relationship

between improvement and land hours per week for sprinters as well as for distance swimmers.

Conclusions reached by the research team were: coaches and athletes should make a decision about increase of land-training workload based on evaluation of relation between workload and performance progression. In some cases, higher strength on land can lead to the reduction of performance because of higher drag in water. The data suggests that sprinters should work not only on land but also on transition from land- to pool-based training by swimming with resistance, surgical tubing, paddles, etc., which is especially important for the older swimmers. Finally, the results showed that the later swimmers started long-term training, the more they tend to work on land training.

Looking to rowing as perhaps the 'closest' sport to swimming in terms of training practice (they do 'on the water' and 'land-based' training), are there any lessons to be learned? The International Rowing Federation (FISA) has published a manual for coaches specifically on the integration of strength training within the overall rowing season. Excerpts from this are relevant to the debate about integrating and periodizing land training for swimming.

On annual planning, the FISA manual states (Nilson, 2001, p. 6):

The year has been divided into 12 months of training. The first month (month 1) is the month immediately after the end of the season. Usually the targeted or peak competition concludes the rowing season. Therefore, month 12 should be the peak competition, the national championships, the regional championship or the World Championships. You should decide on the peak competition for each rower and count backwards to establish the number of the relevant months of training. If the World Championships is the peak competition and it is in September, then October is month one. This programme divides the year into six main phases.

These are guidelines for all rowers across the world, not just the élite, and they give a framework for the coaches to plan their training. On the subject of land-training objectives (Nilson, 2001, p. 7):

> In months 4 and 5 you will find one endurance strength training session each week. These months are usually the coldest and darkest months of winter; therefore endurance fitness can also be developed in the weight lifting room. Muscular Endurance is developed using a lower intensity (40 to 50 per cent of 1 repetition max) and a high number of repetitions. The recovery period is relatively short to obtain an optimal circulatory and muscular training effect. The speed of movement is similar to the stroke rate used during rowing endurance outings. A high number of repetitions (600 to 1,100 repetitions) are necessary to obtain an optimal effect.

This may appear to be overly prescriptive, but individual coaches undoubtedly interpret this outline in their own way with individualized programmes. Further making the point about this important relationship (Nilson, 2001, p. 8):

> Maximal strength is the determining component for peak force production during the rowing race. Gains in maximal strength need a high intensity programme (80 to 95 per cent), a low number of repetitions, and a relatively high number of sets with a recovery period between each set. The total number of repetitions during one training session varies between 220 and 240.

The simplicity of the process is neatly summed up by author John McArthur, who states (McArthur, 1997, p. 108):

> You accept that you cannot hope to improve all of the training elements at the same time. It is clear that you must devise some sort of prioritized structure incorporating everything you want to achieve.

I am not trying to say that rowing and swimming are identical or that there are better (or worse) transfers from land to water in either of them. This is a complex and difficult issue to pin down, but there does appear to be a much stronger emphasis on the prescription and integration of water- and land-based training. This 'holy grail' is never fully referred to in any swimming coaching literature, and Chapter 2 of this book attempts to suggest a way forward for coaches in the effective integration of land- and pool-based training. Perhaps the issue is implicit in swimming coaching circles but, in my experience, the difficult problems of properly integrating land and pool training are usually solved by the actions of one coach recently interviewed when he admitted that if the swimmers were too tired from the training load he just told them to 'miss weight training'. Hardly an integrated, periodized system designed to maximize performance!

In concluding this commentary on land training and its usefulness to swimming performance, it is pertinent to consider the possibility of a paradigm-shift in training practice. The essence of this shift has been alluded to in part already, but some further detail is required. 'Old' thinking meant that coaches considered questions like: How can I get my swimmers stronger in order to swim

*Fig. 8. Contemporary land training.*

faster? 'New' thinking requires coaches to consider issues such as: What can my swimmers not do in the water? How can I design a land- and pool-based programme to improve this? For example, 'old' thinking might mean that a coach concludes that a butterfly swimmer needs more strength to pull them through the water faster and designs a weight-training programme to strengthen the arms, chest and shoulders. 'New' thinking might mean that the coach observes the same swimmer in the pool and sees that they have poor mobility in their lumbar spine, which is preventing them from generating power through the stroke. A dryland programme is then designed (with input from physiotherapists, conditioning experts and the swimming coach) to loosen the lumbar spine, strengthen the stabilizing and postural muscles, and give a base for generating more power in the pool. Very few land-training programmes emanate from this starting point. Of course, the demands made on the lumbar spine will be different for a male/female swimmer, a 50/100/200m swimmer and an age-group/senior swimmer. These factors must also be taken into consideration in designing an appropriate programme for improvement.

Another difference in this contemporary approach is the inclusion of land-based exercises that are multi-directional, i.e. not always in the same plane, and challenging to the core stability of the body. For example, fatigue in the pool may not be exclusively the result of physiological deficiencies like inefficient use of VO2max. The lack of conditioning in postural and alignment musculature may contribute to poor body position, resulting in increased frontal drag and an increased overall work rate. The challenge for the coach therefore is to design an appropriate land-training programme that will allow for improvements in conditioning of the relevant muscles and then a transfer of these gains into swimming performance. Critics of land training, such as Professors Rushall and Costill, would argue that this is best done in the pool. Supporters of this paradigm-shift in land-training practice would argue that a blend of work in and out of the pool is best.

The following article first appeared in *Swimming Technique* and was also reprinted in the book *Swimming Dynamics*. Its author, Cecil Colwin, has written the foreword to this book and is the foremost swimming historian and writer in the world today. He gave permission for this article to be used again here and I feel that it neatly sums up the basic messages of this opening chapter; namely, that land training has featured in the training programmes of swimmers for many years and that coaches have always believed that it is an essential component of successful swimming performance.

### Kiphuth's Cathedral of Sweat
*by Cecil Colwin*

Whenever I see swimmers doing their land training exercises, I think of my friend, the late Bob Kiphuth of Yale, the acknowledged 'Father of Land Training for Swimmers'. His full name and title was Professor Robert John Herman Kiphuth, Director of the Payne Whitney Gymnasium, Yale University. But to us, the great Olympic coach was plain Bob Kiphuth – although any familiarity, during working hours, ended there. Kiphuth ruled Payne Whitney with a rod of iron. The essence of charm outside the gym, Kiphuth's manner changed as soon as he passed through those Gothic portals. Without doubt, Kiphuth was what today's sport psychologists would call an 'authoritarian' coach. Woe betide anyone who had not completed a Kiphuth assignment, or the person who left the steam-room door open, or the swimmer who swam without showering first. On one occasion, a swimmer swam down the pool and sat down in the shallow end. 'If you want to take a bath, bring a cake of soap with you!' bellowed Kiphuth's big baritone voice.

While Kiphuth made many great technical contributions to swimming, his greatest gift to the sport was an abstract one. Through sheer force of intellect and the example he set, he created a new image of the swimming coach, as opposed to the then existing one of a bathrobe-clad-'swimming bum'. Kiphuth always wore a suit, and herringbone tweeds were his favourites. On the Yale campus, his blue fedora hat with its jaunty pheasant feather trimming was his trademark. The 12-floor Gothic structure that was the Payne Whitney Gymnasium was known to generations of Yale students as 'Kiphuth's Cathedral of Sweat'. He made swimming coaching a well-respected profession. He wrote four books, all of them best sellers. His books on land exercises, *Swimming* and *How to be Fit*, converted swimmers worldwide to his new system. In the water, Kiphuth introduced a training method, 'wind sprints', which the Australians developed into interval training still in use today.

Kiphuth started as a physical training instructor in 1917, and was Professor Emeritus of Physical Education when he died in 1967. His kingdom was the beautiful $20,000 Payne Whitney Gymnasium donated by the New York philanthropist of the same name. Beneath its towers many of the world's greatest swimmers trained in the third-floor 50-metre practice pool, and then shattered world records in the basement Payne Whitney Exhibition pool before 1,500 spectators in a theatre-type arena. More world records were broken in this pool than in any other pool in the world.

Early in his career, Kiphuth noted that many swimmers had excellent technique but lacked the muscular strength and power needed to follow through in the fatigue stage of a race. He also believed that training on land conditioned swimmers much quicker than an equivalent time spent in the water. While today's gymnasiums are equipped with advanced and often expensive exercise machines, it was Kiphuth's initial concept that was to lay the foundation for the modern development of this important phase of training. Kiphuth maintained that flexibility was 'a decided asset for a swimmer, in fact practically a necessity'. Kiphuth's exercises were directed to those muscles mainly involved in the propulsive movements of the arms and legs, and also the muscles involved in providing good body position in the water. Kiphuth knew more about the human body in motion than any one I've met. Unknown to most swimming people, Kiphuth co-authored an authoritative tome on the diagnosis and treatment of postural defects. His co-author was Winthrop M. Phelps, son of Williams Lyon Phelps, the great American literary figure. 'Lithe, lean and lasting. That's the way I like them,' Kiphuth would say as he fine-trained his swimmers in the gym.

When I arrived at Yale, early in 1952, to study his methods, I mentioned that I was particularly keen to observe his land-training workouts. 'So you are keen to sample my land workouts?' he said, his steel-blue eyes boring right through to the back of my skull. My heart sank. How could I be so base as to refuse my host's hospitality? Within the hour, there I was, five years retired from swimming and never a workout since, clad in nothing but shorts, duly 'signed up' for one long month of torment under a world-recognized master of torture. Kiphuth appeared through the doorway. 'Good afternoon, gentlemen,' he boomed in his rich baritone, sounding for all the world like Mr Magoo, the famous cartoon character. He had changed into what was known as 'Bob's grey workout suit', an outfit that resembled a long fleece-lined nightshirt. He had with him his 'dual-purpose' bamboo pole. In the gym he used it to tap out the rhythm of the exercises. On the pool deck it became a harpoon that prodded swimmers who drifted into their turns. 'Catch, swing, throw,' Kiphuth called as we threw the 16-pound medicine ball back and forth to each other in continuous rhythm. My partner was John Marshall, holder of every freestyle record from 200 to the mile. Catching John's every throw was like trying to stop a cannon ball, the momentum each time pushing me back several feet. 'Catch, swing, throw,' Kiphuth kept intoning mercilessly. 'Will the young gentleman from South Africker please pick up the rhythm?' he yelled. Each workout lasted an hour. Twenty minutes of almost non-stop free exercises, 20 minutes of medicine ball work, then 20 minutes on the pulley weight machines. These exercises were clever-ly designed, or should I say diabolically designed, to increase muscular strength and power, endurance and flexibility.

Kiphuth's methods were highly successful. He coached many famous champions, including Alan Ford who was only 5-feet, 9-inches and weighed a sparse 150 pounds, yet became the first man to beat 50 seconds for the 100 yards. Other great swimmers such as Olympic champions, Jimmy McLane, Alan Stack, multi-world-record holder John Marshall of Australia, Jeff Farrell, and many more, helped Kiphuth's Yale Teams to win 200 consecutive dual meets. Kiphuth was the 1932, 1936 and 1948 American Olympic coach. At the first post-war Olympics in London, 1948, Kiphuth's US Men's team won every event, the only team in history to do so. His bullet head, bull shoulders, and booming baritone voice were part of the Yale scene for exactly 50 years. On a campus of world famous scholars and athletes, he was 'Mr Yale'.

# CHAPTER 2

# Principles and Planning

## PERIODIZATION

Training plans evolve from general objectives through a series of stages to the most specific objectives. Each level of planning should fit into the next, providing a framework for key programme decisions. It is best to document and review your plans from time to time to assess what progress has been made. Planning must take into account a number of variables, which may, or may not, be under the direct control of the coach. Considerations such as pool access, land-training facilities, squad numbers and the characteristics of squad members will differ from one programme to the next. However, the process of logically constructing both long-term and short-term programmes remains the same. The operation of those plans will naturally differ from one coach to another, based upon individual circumstances. You should first have a basis for long-term programme decisions, i.e. British Swimming's Long-Term Athlete Development (LTAD) framework (explained on pages 27–32). Each coach's philosophy will shape decisions made at every level of planning, but it is useful to have a reference guide for several of the major training parameters – number of pool sessions, volume per session, type and number of land sessions, age/maturation-based training objectives, and so on.

Start with a yearly (or perhaps a two- to three-year cycle would be more appropriate) calendar and target the important competitions that your swimmers are training for. You may need to replicate this exercise for various age-groupings and/or ability levels: for example, swimmers interested only in the social and fitness aspects of sport, swimmers who are very young and still acquiring the background skills/fitness necessary to compete, age-group swimmers with the potential to reach district/county/state qualifying times, age-group swimmers aspiring to compete at the national level, senior swimmers competing at national/international level.

Next, determine the long-term and medium-term preparation requirements for each training level. These requirements must satisfactorily address the background requirements needed for swimmers to achieve their goals (skill, maturation, fitness, competition experience) and the intermediate performance goals that lead up to the major objective, i.e. qualifying meets or performance targets. Coaches must also ask what improvements will be required to reach the major objectives. Are these performance improvements realistic for the age/ability of swimmers in the squad?

Now, based upon the requirements of each training group, determine the single-season

## SEASONAL PLAN

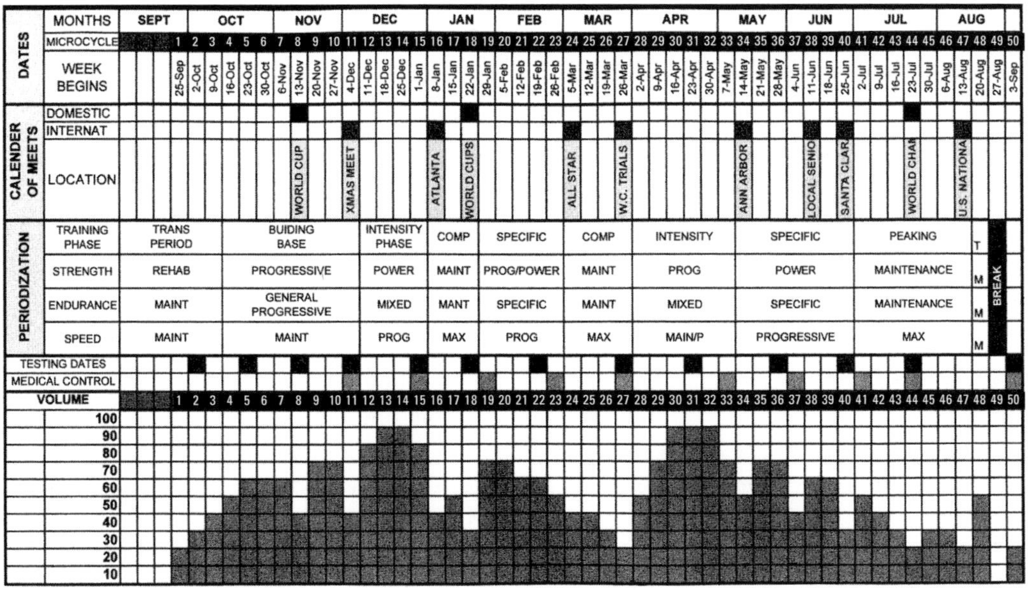

| | SEPT | OCT | NOV | DEC | JAN | FEB | MAR | APR | MAY | JUN | JUL | AUG |
|---|---|---|---|---|---|---|---|---|---|---|---|---|
| **MICROCYCLE** | 1 2 3 4 5 6 | 7 8 9 10 | 11 12 13 14 15 | 16 17 18 19 | 20 21 22 23 | 24 25 26 27 | 28 29 30 31 32 33 | 34 35 36 | 37 38 39 40 | 41 42 43 44 45 | 46 47 48 49 50 | |

**DATES — WEEK BEGINS:** 25-Sep, 2-Oct, 9-Oct, 16-Oct, 23-Oct, 30-Oct, 6-Nov, 13-Nov, 20-Nov, 27-Nov, 4-Dec, 11-Dec, 18-Dec, 25-Dec, 1-Jan, 8-Jan, 15-Jan, 22-Jan, 29-Jan, 5-Feb, 12-Feb, 19-Feb, 26-Feb, 5-Mar, 12-Mar, 19-Mar, 26-Mar, 2-Apr, 9-Apr, 16-Apr, 23-Apr, 30-Apr, 7-May, 14-May, 21-May, 28-May, 4-Jun, 11-Jun, 18-Jun, 25-Jun, 2-Jul, 9-Jul, 16-Jul, 23-Jul, 30-Jul, 6-Aug, 13-Aug, 20-Aug, 27-Aug, 3-Sep

**CALENDAR OF MEETS** — DOMESTIC / INTERNAT

**LOCATION:** WORLD CUP, XMAS MEET, ATLANTA, WORLD CUPS, ALL STAR, W.C. TRIALS, ANN ARBOR, LOCAL SENIOR, SANTA CLAR, WORLD CHAM, U.S. NATIONA

### PERIODIZATION

| | | | | | | | | | | | |
|---|---|---|---|---|---|---|---|---|---|---|---|
| **TRAINING PHASE** | TRANS PERIOD | BUILDING BASE | INTENSITY PHASE | COMP | SPECIFIC | COMP | INTENSITY | SPECIFIC | PEAKING | T |
| **STRENGTH** | REHAB | PROGRESSIVE | POWER | MAINT | PROG/POWER | MAINT | PROG | POWER | MAINTENANCE | M |
| **ENDURANCE** | MAINT | GENERAL PROGRESSIVE | MIXED | MANT | SPECIFIC | MAINT | MIXED | SPECIFIC | MAINTENANCE | M |
| **SPEED** | MAINT | MAINT | PROG | MAX | PROG | MAX | MAIN/P | PROGRESSIVE | MAX | M |

(Right-hand column: BREAK)

**TESTING DATES**

**MEDICAL CONTROL**

**VOLUME** (scale 100, 90, 80, 70, 60, 50, 40, 30, 20, 10) — microcycles 1 to 50

*Fig. 9. An annual macrocycle.*

objectives. A training season may be six to seven months for some swimmers, or a complete year for others. This training 'season' is usually called a 'macrocycle' (*see* Fig. 9). The novice coach may find it difficult to estimate the amount of improvement possible during a season, but experience and help from mentors will help in this regard. Within each season's training there may be several intermediate objectives. The period of time a coach devotes to achieving these objectives (which have a fitness or skill base) is called a 'mesocycle' (*see* Fig. 10). For example, three fundamentals of every training programme are: improvement of aerobic fitness; improvement of speed; and improvement of swimming technique. Attainment of these objectives allows the swimmer to train more specifically to competition objectives. Therefore, specific periods of time during the season must focus on these fundamentals.

However, training must never focus so closely on one fundamental that the others are neglected. Training is always a mixture of several things, usually with at least a primary and a secondary focus. The length of each training cycle will depend upon the major training objective (some objectives take longer than others to achieve). There is also variation within any group of swimmers that determines each athlete's ability to absorb and adapt to the training programme. Physiology texts will suggest that adaptation to specific types of training stimuli will take so many weeks to achieve. However, because most coaches work with a wide range of ages, maturation levels and abilities, it would be difficult to suggest that one plan fits all squad members. The length of any adaptation period is also influenced by each swimmer's training background. For example, mature, senior swimmers, who maintain

| Training Week | Number of Sessions | Average Total Distance (m) | Main Emphasis | Other Notes |
|---|---|---|---|---|
| 1 | 6–8 | 25,000–40,000 | Stroke technique<br>Skill acquisition | Competition?<br>Testing week? |
| 2 | 7–9 | 30,000–50,000 | Kicking/pulling<br>Moderate intensity aerobic endurance | Testing week? |
| 3 | 8–10 | 45,000–80,000 | Moderate intensity aerobic endurance<br>Stroke-specific low intensity | |
| 4 | 9–10 | 55,000–80,000 | Anaerobic threshold<br>Stroke-specific moderate intensity | |
| 5 | 8–10 | 45,000–65,000 | Stroke-specific high intensity<br>    production/tolerance<br>Maximum VO2 | |
| 6 | 7–9 | 30,000–45,000 | Stroke-specific high intensity<br>    production/tolerance<br>Basic speed<br>Race pace | |
| 7 | 6–8 | 15,000–30,000 | Starting and turning skills<br>Basic speed<br>Race preparation – REST | Competition? |

*Fig. 10. A training mesocycle.*

high levels of aerobic fitness from one season to the next, will not require a long period of general training devoted to improving this capacity.

Within each mesocycle most coaches plan each week's training as a measurable training unit or microcycle (*see* Fig. 11). Some full-time coaches of full-time swimmers use slightly smaller units (two to four days) or somewhat longer units (e.g. fourteen days) to fit their plans, especially when using altitude training. Each microcycle contains smaller training units, such as individual training days or training sessions. Planning training programmes within units of time allows the coach to control the application of the stress–recovery–adaptation sequence

of events. Finally, the coach must actually plan and implement each training session. Based upon the planning outline, each training session will be structured to reflect the desired outcomes within that micro–meso–macrocycle.

Every training session will contain these core components:

• Warm-up activities that prepare the swimmer for other types of training (these may also address fitness and skill related objectives);
• Activities specific to one or two primary training objectives (these are training sets designed to achieve some physiological, psychological or tactical objective);

*Fig. 11 A training microcycle.*

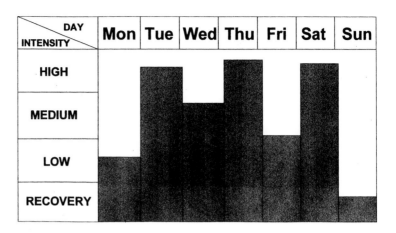

- Activities that contribute to recovery (this may be the traditional swim-down or a set that contributes to primary or secondary training objectives if they happen to be recovery orientated).

You may also wish to include a secondary training set during some (or all) sessions. This type of training set addresses a secondary (minor) objective. Care must be exercised to construct secondary sets that contribute to the overall session, rather than detract from it. Training sets are constructed to define a specific training stress and training sets that target primary objectives must be constructed to a specific intensity and volume consistent with the overall plan. Training sets designed to achieve secondary objectives are usually more varied in their composition and volume.

The major questions every coach must answer (as reflected in the structure of the training programme) include:

- How long should the training season last? (Macrocycle.)
- How many pool and land sessions are appropriate and what am I trying to achieve with this swimmer or group of swimmers? (Mesocycle.)

- How much training volume and intensity is appropriate to each session? (Microcycle.)

For example, an average ten-year-old club swimmer can be expected to handle four pool training sessions per week of one hour duration (or slightly longer) and accomplish somewhere between 2 and 3.5km of training during each session. During the course of a season (which may last up to forty weeks) this swimmer will accumulate around 500km of training background. The various training outcomes, skill objectives, cognitive and competition objectives are all identified within the LTAD framework. However, there may be variation based upon individual ability, maturation or past training history. Some ten-year-old swimmers will respond more like a twelve-year-old and some like an eight-year-old. A young athlete new to the sport may have great physical capacities, but lack the skill components characteristically acquired by others at eight or nine years of age. Therefore, the LTAD framework is used as a guide. It should help the coach identify which developmental areas are on track and which are advanced or behind, but should not be followed slavishly, as a prescriptive tool for all

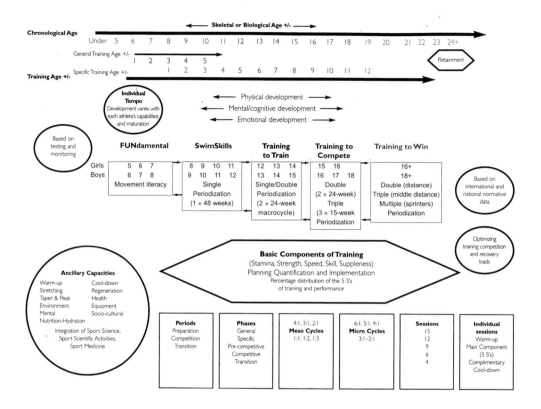

*Fig. 12. LTAD periodization chart.*

planning. Another way to consider the development of swimmers is shown in Fig. 12. At each stage of the LTAD process, the main pool- and land-based training objectives are shown, moving from the very general athletic and movement-oriented activities, towards the highly specific, individually-based programmes of élite performers.

Another example of how the LTAD framework can be used is the evolution of the 'break-point volume' concept, proposed by British Swimming's National Performance Director, Bill Sweetenham. First conceived when he was National Youth Coach in Australia, the concept links age group and senior

swimming through a progressive increase in pool-based training volume to an optimal amount per week. It recognizes the fact that during the maturation years an increased volume of training can be absorbed by the athlete (providing the training intensity is controlled within certain limits). It is much harder, although not impossible, to absorb similar training levels later in the swimmer's career if the proper background training has not taken place. The key ages are 13 to 15 years (±one year), with girls generally responding at a slightly younger age than boys. According to Bill Sweetenham, these five factors are critical to the nature of training:

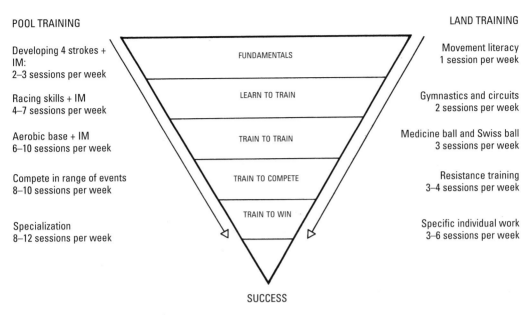

POOL TRAINING

Developing 4 strokes + IM:
2–3 sessions per week

Racing skills + IM
4–7 sessions per week

Aerobic base + IM
6–10 sessions per week

Compete in range of events
8–10 sessions per week

Specialization
8–12 sessions per week

FUNDAMENTALS

LEARN TO TRAIN

TRAIN TO TRAIN

TRAIN TO COMPETE

TRAIN TO WIN

SUCCESS

LAND TRAINING

Movement literacy
1 session per week

Gymnastics and circuits
2 sessions per week

Medicine ball and Swiss ball
3 sessions per week

Resistance training
3–4 sessions per week

Specific individual work
3–6 sessions per week

*Fig. 13. The filtering of performance.*

1. Up to and through maturation the quantity of training under aerobic workloads is more important than the quantity of training under high-intensity workloads (although it is recognized that all types of training are required in a well-balanced programme).
2. After maturation, the proportion of quality (at a high percentage of maximum) training with break-point volume becomes more important to the overall success of the training programme.
3. Recovery is always a major concern in the design of training programmes.
4. Quality technique and application of skills are vitally important, i.e. at all training intensities.
5. The frequency (in terms of the number of sessions and the continuity of those sessions) of training stimulus is important.

The general observation by Sweetenham is that an annual training volume of 2,000–2,500km should be accomplished over a 42- to 46-week training season by the time a swimmer reaches his/her physical maturation, i.e. the 'training to compete' phase of LTAD. This equates to a little over 6km per session in a training plan that averages eight to ten sessions per week. The yearly training volume will remain similar to this in the following years, although the composition of training will change as events and competitions become even more focused. This concept of training fits very well within the LTAD framework, assuming that all necessary progressions through the younger age groups have been satisfied.

## THE SWIMMER PATHWAY

The infrastructure of swimming in Britain has been undergoing significant change in the past few years. Fig. 14 on page 29 illustrates a 'swimmer pathway' from learning to swim right up to élite level. This is also known as the Long-Term Athlete Development model (LTAD model).

LTAD is about achieving optimal training, competition and recovery throughout an athlete's career, particularly in relation to the important growth and development years of young people. If a long-term approach to training is not adopted, there is likely to be a plateau in performance when growth and development slows significantly, which for some swimmers may result in their performances getting worse. At this point, the short-term training approach cannot be reversed. This often leads to drop-out before a swimmer has achieved close to their potential.

The ASA and Sport England (the national agency for promoting and developing sport) state that there are five clear reasons for introducing a LTAD approach:

1. To establish a clear swimmer-development pathway.
2. To identify gaps in the current swimmer-development pathway.
3. To realign and integrate the programmes for developing swimmers and swimming in Britain.
4. To provide a planning tool, based on scientific research, for coaches and administrators.
5. To guide planning for optimal performance.

The following are some general observations of sporting systems from around the world (including Britain): young athletes under-train and over-compete; there are low training to competition ratios in the early years of development; adult competitions are superimposed on young athletes; adult training programmes are superimposed on young athletes; male programmes are superimposed on females; training in the early years focuses on outcomes (winning) rather than processes (optimal training); chronological age influences coaching rather than biological age; the 'critical' periods of accelerated adaptation are not fully utilized; poor training between six and sixteen years of age cannot be fully corrected (athletes will never reach genetic potential); the best coaches are encouraged to work at élite level; coach education tends to skim the growth, development and maturation of young people; coaches, swimmers and parents need to be educated in LTAD principles; administrators and officials need to be educated in LTAD principles.

LTAD is a sports development framework that is based on human growth and development. In short, it is about adopting an athlete-centred approach to swimming development. All young people follow the same pattern of growth from infancy through adolescence, but there are significant individual differences in both the timing and magnitude of the changes that take place. It is, however, important to stress that human growth and development happens without training, although swimming training can enhance all of the changes that take place. Research tells us that there are critical periods in the life of a young person in which the effects of training can be maximized. This has led to the notion that young people should be exposed to specific types of training during periods of rapid growth and that the types of training should change with the patterns of growth. These have been used to devise a five-stage LTAD framework that has been adapted to swimming:

1. FUNdamentals – basic movement literacy.
2. SwimSkills – building technique.
3. Training to Train – building the engine.
4. Training to Compete – optimizing the engine.
5. Training to Win – top performance.

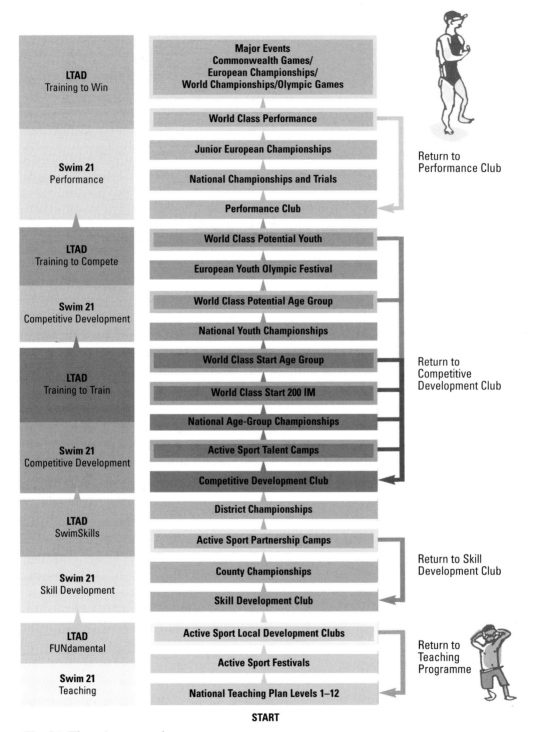

| LTAD<br>Training to Win | **Major Events**<br>**Commonwealth Games/**<br>**European Championships/**<br>**World Championships/Olympic Games** | |
| --- | --- | --- |
| | **World Class Performance** | |
| Swim 21<br>Performance | **Junior European Championships** | Return to<br>Performance Club |
| | **National Championships and Trials** | |
| | **Performance Club** | |
| LTAD<br>Training to Compete | **World Class Potential Youth** | |
| | **European Youth Olympic Festival** | |
| Swim 21<br>Competitive Development | **World Class Potential Age Group** | |
| | **National Youth Championships** | |
| LTAD<br>Training to Train | **World Class Start Age Group** | Return to<br>Competitive<br>Development Club |
| | **World Class Start 200 IM** | |
| | **National Age-Group Championships** | |
| Swim 21<br>Competitive Development | **Active Sport Talent Camps** | |
| | **Competitive Development Club** | |
| LTAD<br>SwimSkills | **District Championships** | |
| | **Active Sport Partnership Camps** | Return to Skill<br>Development Club |
| Swim 21<br>Skill Development | **County Championships** | |
| | **Skill Development Club** | |
| LTAD<br>FUNdamental | **Active Sport Local Development Clubs** | |
| | **Active Sport Festivals** | Return to<br>Teaching<br>Programme |
| Swim 21<br>Teaching | **National Teaching Plan Levels 1–12** | |

**START**

*Fig. 14. The swimmer pathway.*

## Stage 1: FUNdamentals (Girls 5–8 Years; Boys 6–9 Years)

The FUNdamentals stage should be structured and fun. The emphasis is on developing basic movement literacy and fundamental movement skills. The skills to be developed are the ABCs (agility, balance, co-ordination and speed), RJT (running, jumping and throwing), KGBs (kinesthetics, gliding, buoyancy and striking with the body) and CKs (catching, kicking and striking with an implement). In order to develop basic movement literacy successfully, participation in as many sports as possible should be encouraged. Speed, power and endurance should be developed using FUN and games. In addition, children should be introduced to the simple rules and ethics of sports. No periodization should take place, but there should be well-structured programmes with proper progressions that are monitored regularly.

## Stage 2: SwimSkills (Girls 8–11 Years; Boys 9–12 Years)

During this stage, young swimmers should learn how to train and develop the skills of a specific sport. There may be participation in complementary sports, i.e. those sports that use similar energy systems and movement patterns. They should also learn the basic technical/tactical skills, and ancillary capacities:

• Warm up and cool down;
• Stretching;
• Hydration and nutrition;
• Recovery;
• Relaxation and focusing.

This stage coincides with peak motor co-ordination. Therefore there should be an emphasis on skill development. Training should also include the use of 'own body weight' exercises; medicine ball and Swiss ball exercises, as well as developing suppleness. Although the focus is on training, competition should be used to test and refine skills. The recommended training-to-competition ratio is 75 to 25 per cent. If a young swimmer misses this stage of development then he/she will never reach their full potential. One of the main reasons that athletes plateau during the later stages of their careers is an over-emphasis on competition instead of optimizing training during this very important stage.

## Stage 3: Training to Train (Girls 11–14 Years; Boys 12–15 Years)

During the Training to Train stage, there should be an emphasis on aerobic conditioning. This is the stage where there is greater individualization of fitness and technical training. The focus should still be on training rather than competition and the training should be predominantly of high-volume, low-intensity workloads. It is important to emphasize that high-volume, low-intensity training cannot be achieved in a limited time period, and therefore the time commitment to training should increase significantly. As the volume of training increases there is likely to be a reduction in the number of competitions undertaken. However, there should now be specific targets for each competition undertaken with a view to learning basic tactics and mental preparation.

During this stage, training should continue to develop suppleness and to include the use of 'own body weight' exercises; medicine ball and Swiss ball exercises. However, towards the end of this stage, preparations should be made for the development of strength, which for girls occurs at the end of this stage and for boys at the beginning of the next stage. This

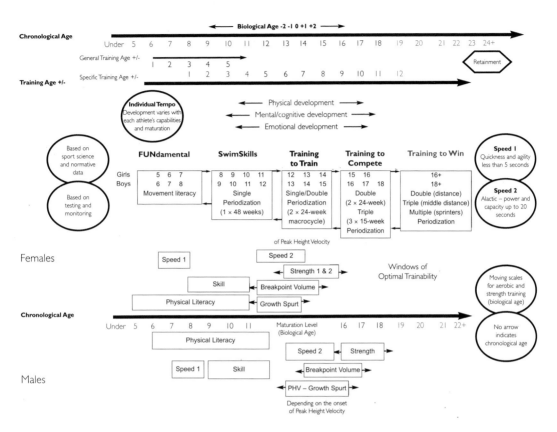

*Fig. 15. LTAD trainability chart.*

should include learning correct strength-training techniques. The ancillary capacities (the knowledge-base of how to warm up and warm down; how to stretch and when to stretch; how to optimize nutrition and hydration; mental preparation; regeneration; how and when to taper and peak; pre-competition, competition and post-competition routines) should be established.

Similar to the previous stage, if insufficient time is devoted to this stage or it is missed, then the young swimmer will never reach their full potential.

## Stage 4: Training to Compete (Girls 14–16 Years; Boys 15–18 Years)

During the Training to Compete stage there should be a continued emphasis on physical conditioning with the focus on maintaining high-volume workloads but with increasing intensity. The number of competitions should be similar to the end of the previous stage but the emphasis should be on developing individual strengths and weaknesses through modelling and nurturing technical and tactical skills based around specific strokes or distances, but not both. As a result, there should be either double or triple periodization of the training year. In addition, the ancillary capacities should be refined so they are more specific to the individual's needs. During this stage, training should also focus on developing maximum strength and power gains through the use of land training. This should be coupled with continued work on core body strength and maintaining flexibility.

## Stage 5: Training to Win (Females: 16-plus Years; Males: 18-plus Years)

This is the final stage of preparation. The emphasis should be on specialization and performance enhancement. All of the athletes' physical, technical, tactical, mental and ancillary capacities should now be fully established with the focus shifting to the optimization of performance. Athletes should be trained to peak for specific competitions and major events. Therefore, all aspects of training should be individualized for specific events. There should be either double or triple periodization, depending on the events being trained for.

An illustration of the complexity of the LTAD process is shown in Fig. 15 on page 31.

## TRAINING OBJECTIVES

The planning process outlined above makes reference to training objectives at every stage. Successful planning incorporates all of the coach's conceptual models, i.e. physiological, technical and psychological. The greatest mistake made by most coaches is their failure to look at the total picture and keep that picture in perspective with the age and ability of their swimmers. This is sometimes referred to as 'the performance puzzle' and is shown in Fig. 16. In particular, many coaches do not consider the integration of land training within this 'big picture', something that is dealt with in detail later in this section. Planning a training programme for very young swimmers is therefore very clear, because the primary objectives of training are very narrowly defined. Skill development, aerobic capacity and having fun are the primary objectives; maintaining natural speed and developing race skills are the secondary objectives. The complexity of the objectives (or lack of complexity in this case) determines the amount of detail that the coach needs to plan.

Young swimmers do not require large variation in the training plan from one cycle to the next because their training needs are simple. Good advice for coaches working with very young swimmers is to devote most of your planning to skills across all four strokes and IM (Individual Medley) and general aerobic fitness based on an IM programme. Also, learn how to construct many different training sets that may look different but that achieve the same physiological objective. In terms of land training, the emphasis should be on general aerobic conditioning, fun games and teaching the key skills and techniques to be used in later, more demanding training cycles. Activities like Swiss-ball work and core-stability exercises are applicable throughout a swimmer's career and should be initiated at this early stage.

During the years in which swimmers experience their most rapid physical changes (*see* the 'windows of optimal trainability' in Fig. 15), the complexity of training variables changes. In the pool, consolidation of technique and continued increases in aerobic capacity are still the most important objectives, but factors such as muscle strength to body weight ratio, speed and acceleration, and training volume/intensity must also be addressed in the training plan. On land, the

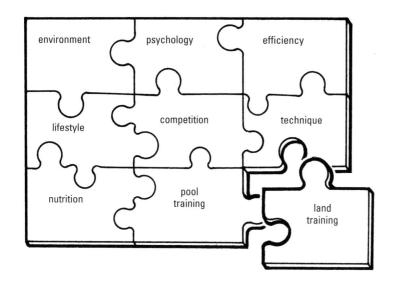

*Fig. 16. The performance puzzle.*

emphasis should be on improving specific functional strength to be applied in the pool and on developing a platform of sound training habits and routines.

Yet, there are still training variables that should be held in reserve for older age-groupers and senior swimmers. For example, pre-pubertal swimmers will probably increase their aerobic capacity more through maturation and appropriate amounts of training at/near OBLA (Onset of Blood Lactate Accumulation) speeds than from frequent exposure to high-intensity VO2 training sets. Young swimmers will improve pure speed by perfecting technique and core-body strength. Large volumes (as a percentage of the total work accomplished) of high-intensity training sets will wear the swimmer down and can be harmful to overall development. Coaches often over-estimate the progress of swimmers aged ten to twelve years and begin to train them like mini-adults; resulting in the application of an unrealistic programme and possibly the loss of many swimmers to other sports altogether. Training objectives for girls aged 12 to 13 and boys aged 13 to 14 begin

to change dramatically because their needs are more complex. Provided that earlier training has given these swimmers the correct background in technique and aerobic capacity, etc., there are many new training objectives, which must be included in the coach's plan. The emphasis on training volume and intensity, and how they interact, must be carefully reviewed at this stage of a swimmer's career. Anaerobic capacity begins to take on greater importance and subtle changes are brought into the complexity of the training plan. There is still awareness that maturational changes are incomplete, very few 12- to 13-year-olds reflect the characteristics of senior swimmers and the coach must be able to recognize signs of maturity and adjust his/her programme for both advanced, as well as late-maturing, individuals. A good way of managing and organizing land training at this stage of development is through the use of circuit training (*see* Chapter 3 for details). The advantage of this form of training is that it keeps groups together, but still allows individual variations according to specific need and ability.

Planning training for most mid age-group swimmers (14 to 16 years old) is closer again to that of senior swimmers, with the exception that recovery mechanisms are still very robust for the younger swimmers in this category. As a general rule, these teenagers (particularly the girls) will be able to absorb large volumes of work. Planning the desired emphasis of training volume and training intensity becomes the greatest challenge for the coach. The more talented swimmers will now be getting ready to make the transition to higher levels of competition. At this time the coach must be able to assess if there are significant weaknesses present in the swimmer's training profile. In fact, at every stage of a swimmer's development the coach must assess the relative strengths/weaknesses and plan to fill the gaps left from earlier stages or correct potential problems, i.e. before they become limitations for a senior swimmer. Training complexity is again expanded because competition objectives begin to narrow. During the early years of a swimmer's career there is relatively equal emphasis on the development of all strokes and most competition distances; from the mid-teen years the swimmer begins to specialize more. The coach must respond with more specific programmes every year; this requires more detailed planning. On dry land, the fact that pool-training loads have increased is something that must now become a major consideration. Questions such as when to do the land training (before or after pool sessions), how often to do the sessions (per week, etc.), and what balance to give to the training (types and intensities of sessions), is now a fundamental part of the periodization process.

The complexity of objectives in the training programme for senior swimmers and/or élite swimmers is enormous. Higher levels of competition create different demands on the swimmer in every aspect of performance, i.e. nutrition, mental skills, strength/flexibility, physiological preparation, technical preparation and so on. Although most coaches (particularly novice coaches) do not train élite level swimmers, the training plans designed for these élite athletes are usually the ones every coach wants to study and emulate. Learning from the success or experience of others is important, but learning why and how those results were achieved is perhaps more important. Almost every élite swimmer can trace his/her training history through a similar process of successfully achieving age-related training objectives. Planning and seeing the whole picture are the keys to a coach's success.

## TRAINING MODELS

The coach can effectively plan training if he/she has a model to follow. The training model explained here presents five ways in which a swimmer's individual abilities are affected by training. The model directs the coach to plan training activities with:

- An ever-present concern for the development and application of optimal stroke technique and competition skills;
- The realization that energy supply comes from three metabolic pathways and that each responds to different training demands, and all three must be continually developed and maintained;
- A knowledge that the impact of physical and psychological stresses are interactive – neither can be ignored or separated from the other;
- An understanding of the changes that occur within the body as a response to the type and amount of stress; and
- The acceptance of two basic training principles: adaptation and progressive overload.

The initial discussion centres on training in general, but a more specific exploration of how land and pool training could be integrated follows.

## Early-Season Objectives

At the start of any season the training objectives are:

- To build a solid physiological base from which more specific work can be constructed;
- To develop or consolidate the techniques and skills that are appropriate for that age/ability swimmer;
- To assess a number of general strengths or weaknesses and plan appropriate training strategies.

Stroke technique and skills will be primary objectives during every phase of training, but perhaps more emphasis is placed on these at the start of a season. Increasing aerobic fitness will be the primary physiological objective, with pure speed and race speed as secondary objectives. Therefore, the types of training used most often during the early stages of a season should be: aerobic base, aerobic endurance and critical speed (primary objectives); maximum speed and sprint capacity (secondary objectives). The early-season phase of a programme might consist of only one or two larger training cycles. For example, the first cycle might be a general training period consisting of six smaller (weekly) cycles of successively increasing training volume. A variation on this might be two weeks of increasing volume, one week reduction in volume (recovery week) repeated.

Once the majority of swimmers begin to show signs of adaptation to general fitness training (evidenced through the use of training sets) a second larger cycle of aerobic capacity

training would follow. The pattern of increasing the overall training stress during successive smaller units of time (microcycles) or using a build-up/recovery pattern is repeated. Although endurance remains the main focus of the programme, the relative amount of each type of training will change to meet the build-up or recovery demands within that cycle. Therefore, in this example, early season might be defined as a mesocycle of twelve weeks of training through August–October. Naturally the length of any one phase of the season is dependent upon the length of the total training season and the rate of adaptation, i.e. swimmers having a high level of fitness at the start of the cycle may not need a long general/endurance preparation phase.

How do we know if the primary and secondary training objectives are being achieved? Repeated testing of various physiological capacities and race times help us to effectively monitor the training programme. A practical and useful system is to administer test sets that are specific to the training objectives. Documenting improvements in training and racing performance should give the coach and swimmer confidence that the training plan is working. The coach should also administer relevant tests for each of the secondary objectives. If performance characteristics of secondary objectives decline substantially (in this case of an endurance phase of training, the secondary objectives are maximum speed and sprint speed), then the coach may have placed too much emphasis on a single type of training. However, it is also unrealistic to expect top sprint performance when concentrated endurance work remains the major focus of training. A swimmer's speed will be depressed somewhat, but this should respond to the cyclic nature of the training programme, i.e. variation in the amount of recovery and sprinting in relation to endurance loads. A simple test of maximum speed, such as 6 × 25m on a 2-minute interval (easy swimming between efforts) checking times, stroke rate and stroke counts, should be administered regularly (even during endurance training periods). Changes in maximum speed are evaluated on the basis of the average time, as well as the best time; some coaches may vary this test by timing six repeat swims and recording the best four times. By also measuring stroke efficiency parameters, coaches can track all the improvements made throughout the season.

## Mid-Season Objectives

Mid-season might be loosely defined as the second major phase of the season, consisting of one or more large training mesocycles (November–January in the UK). The key to a successful progression in the training programme is to maintain all the performance gains of earlier cycles, while building performance gains in other areas. During this phase of the season, swimmers will regularly participate in competitions. Depending on the season's objectives, the coach must plan training around or through these competitions.

The characteristic feature of mid-season planning is the way the coach manipulates volume and intensity within the training programme. It is very likely that the training volume from week-to-week is sustained at a volume that is less than the peak volume reached when endurance was the focus. However, the overall training stress during mid-season is usually greater because volume and intensity variables have shifted. The progressive overload principle has been applied by increasing the total loading (stress) from one week to the next through a period of weeks, and then allowing a reduction in the loading (recovery) to facilitate adaptation. The most common representation of this process is known as the 'supercompensation curve', shown in Fig. 17. The exercise stimulus is the session or main set and the real art in designing training programmes is to initiate the next set/session before the body returns to the baseline. This is what effective coaches do all the time.

The number of the progressive loading cycles (sessions) planned will depend upon the ability of swimmers to recover sufficiently on a day-to-day basis. Fig. 18 shows three examples of how this arrangement of training can be done. If training is sequenced inappropriately, as shown in example (c) in Fig. 18, i.e. before the body has compensated, the results will be the opposite of those desired. When we come to discuss the integration of land- and pool-based training later, this becomes absolutely crucial in the overall planning process. Generally, 2:1, 3:1 or sometimes 4:1 loading patterns, i.e. load : recovery cycles, are used as a basis for planning. The composition of training during a recovery cycle must be carefully planned. It is inefficient simply to rest passively, unless recovering from illness or injury. As a general rule the volume of work during a recovery cycle is set at 50–60 per cent of the volume of previous loading cycles, but the content of the programme is such that residual fatigue (from one session to the next) is greatly reduced or eliminated. A recovery week will contain fast and/or quality swimming, as long as the overall amount of stress is reduced. Mid-season objectives are evaluated from competition results as well as test sets. It is valuable for coaches to record more information than just an overall race time to assess progress in various technical/tactical areas. These may be race specific variables such as:

- Time from the starting signal until the swimmer's head passes the 15m mark;
- Stroke count and stroke rate during each 25m-segment of a race;
- Split times to judge pacing;

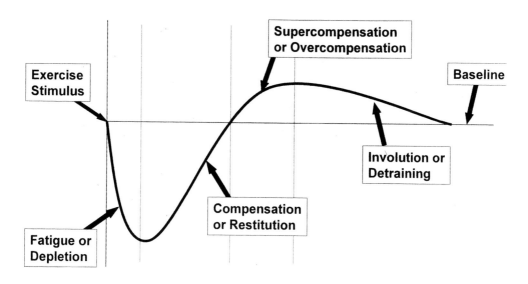

Fig. 17. The supercompensation curve.

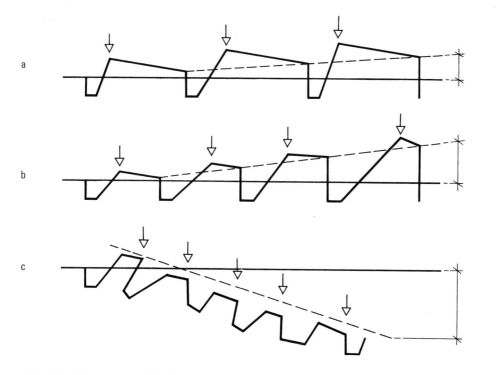

Fig. 18. The pattern of daily training.

- Turn time, i.e. as the head passes under the backstroke flags until the head passes the same point on the return lap;
- Time and distance underwater at the start and off each turn (this is particularly important for breaststrokers);
- Finish time, i.e. from the flags to the wall; and, of course,
- Stroke counting and stroke rates per lap.

Because the intensity of training increases during the mid-season phase, the coach must be acutely aware of how day-to-day training objectives are programmed. There will be several concurrent types of training programmed into each session and sequenced into the microcycle. Some of the training outcomes will produce residual fatigue effects and, if repeated too often, these high-stress training methods may overcome the swimmer's ability to recover. This is not to say that full recovery is always desirable from one training session to the next, i.e. the progressive overload principle must be applied. However, coaches must monitor short-term recovery while scheduling training loads that will stimulate adaptation to higher levels of performance.

### Late-Season Objectives

Naturally, the overall focus of any season's training is the performances achieved in the end competition. The final phase of a season consists of at least one larger cycle(s) to conclude the preparation. In the UK this would normally be one leading up to the major trials event in March/April and then a further mesocycle towards the main summer event(s). The final portion of this cycle is known as a taper, during which swimmers must be ready to perform to their full potential (*see* Chapter 4 for full details of tapering and the place of land training within it). The function of a taper, which may include two, three, four or more weeks, is to allow the athlete's body to over-compensate by:

- Increasing rest and opportunities for regeneration of muscle tissue;
- Mentally focusing on peak performance; and
- Allowing adaptations to the mechanisms involved in energy production.

The physiological outcomes during the taper, reflect complex training effects. As mentioned earlier, young age-group swimmers should follow a very simple pattern of training objectives. Therefore, it is probably not necessary for the coach to plan a detailed taper for swimmers under the age of 12 years. During the rapid-growth years the taper cycle may be more of a rehearsal for future years than a specific benefit to the current state of competition readiness. Swimmers at this age generally recover quickly and completely during a relatively short period of time (one to two weeks). Long taper periods used on junior athletes effectively reduce the amount of training time available during the season. It is better to use the available time to lengthen either the preparation or specific training phases (further details on how to incorporate land training in the taper are given later in this section).

Swimmers participating in the full taper process will require progressively more rest during each microcycle of the taper. The coach must ensure that a reduction in total training volume does not represent the elimination of lower intensity aerobic swimming. Fitness must be maintained throughout the taper. Too great a reduction in aerobic loads may result in the proportion of high-intensity swimming becoming too great (as part of the total training load). High-intensity or quality swimming must remain in the training programme throughout the taper; however, the volume of this high-stress work is gradually reduced and recovery between stresses becomes more complete. Although the coach has given detailed attention to stroke technique and race strategy throughout the season, these skills are refined during the taper. Some elements of the training programme, such as specific strength-training exercises, are eliminated during the taper because the effects of this training should already have been realized. Other elements, such as stretchcords, swimbench and mental-skills training, continue at the same loading. Key training sets involving high to very high intensity are either reduced in volume or modified, so that recovery between individual swims is enhanced.

Swimmers who train twice daily usually progressively reduce (in each week of the taper) the number of training sessions attended. This should not always be the early morning sessions, as most big meets will require swimmers to perform at, or close to, their best in the morning heats. Because the objectives of a taper are so complex, there are numerous considerations that must be addressed by the coach. For a fuller explanation of the physical and psychological aspects of the tapering process, *see Crowood Sports Guides: Swimming*, Chapter 19.

**Transition Periods**

At the end of a season or championship competition, a transition period exists. Current evidence suggests that complete rest, i.e. no swim training at all, is a less effective option than a specific transition-training programme. The greatest stressors during and following a major competition are psychological, not physical. The physiological adaptations made during a season will gradually be lost if no fitness work is done. Therefore, the primary training objective must be to mentally refresh the swimmer while providing a sufficient training load. Remember that once a high level of aerobic fitness is achieved, the training load required to retain minimum race fitness becomes much less. During a post-taper period the coach should schedule one to two weeks of low-intensity aerobic work, mixed with sets of short sprints (the number of sessions per week being 50–60 per cent of the peak season load) as a transition into the next training cycle.

Introducing innovative and interesting alternative training activities may also satisfy the swimmer's psychological needs. If swimmers require a more complete break from the pool, the coach may introduce cross-training as an alternative to limited pool training. Cross-training is non-specific training that includes a variety of sports activities outside the pool. In this context cross-training has two major objectives:

1. Maintenance of aerobic fitness;
2. Increase in overall muscular strength.

Some caution should be exercised to ensure swimmers protect themselves from potential injury in sports where they may not be highly skilled. Otherwise, active participation in other sports will help to refresh the swimmer mentally, and to maintain the swimmer physically.

**Examples of Microcycle Planning**

It would be impossible to illustrate every combination of training, i.e. based upon age, maturity, ability, and training phase of the season suitable within a weekly plan. However, based upon the principles outlined, a few examples of weekly training plans are presented overleaf. The possible composition of individual training sets is infinite and therefore no specific examples are given. The key objectives relevant to training-session design are presented as either a major or minor focus of each session plan.

| DAY / DATE | MONDAY | TUESDAY | WEDNESDAY | THURSDAY | FRIDAY | SATURDAY | SUNDAY |
|---|---|---|---|---|---|---|---|
| **A.M.** | | | | | | IM aerobic | |
| [SUBSET] | | | | | | F/c drills | |
| Distance | | | | | | 2.2 | |
| **P.M.** | | IM aerobic | | Im aerobic | | | |
| [SUBSET] | | F/c kick | | B/c drills | | | |
| Distance | | 2.5 | | 2.3 | | | |
| **LAND** | | | | Games & Gym (post swim) | | 10min Run (pre swim) | |
| **DAILY TOTAL** | 0.0 | 2.5 | 0.0 | 2.3 | 0.0 | 2.2 | DAY OFF |
| | | | | | | **WEEKLY TOTAL** | 7.0 |

(a) A FUNdamentals microcycle

| DAY / DATE | MONDAY | TUESDAY | WEDNESDAY | THURSDAY | FRIDAY | SATURDAY | SUNDAY |
|---|---|---|---|---|---|---|---|
| **A.M.** | | | | | | A2 IM swim | |
| [SUBSET] | | | | | | Speed All strokes | |
| Distance | | | | | | 3.5 | |
| **P.M.** | A1/A2 IM swim | A1/A2 F/c swim | A2 B/c swim | A2 IM swim | | | |
| [SUBSET] | F/c drills | IM kick | F/c kick | Fly drills | | | |
| Distance | 3.2 | 3.5 | 3.3 | 3.6 | | | |
| **LAND** | | | Circuits (pre swim) | | | 20min Run (post swim) | |
| **DAILY TOTAL** | 3.2 | 3.5 | 3.3 | 3.6 | 0.0 | 3.5 | DAY OFF |
| | | | | | | **WEEKLY TOTAL** | 17.1 |

(b) A SwimSkills microcycle

| DAY / DATE | MONDAY | TUESDAY | WEDNESDAY | THURSDAY | FRIDAY | SATURDAY | SUNDAY |
|---|---|---|---|---|---|---|---|
| **A.M.** | | | A1/A2 B/c swim | | A1 IM drill/swim | VO2 No1 swim | |
| [SUBSET] | | | Stroke drills | | | A1 recovery | |
| Distance | | | 4.5 | | | 6.3 | |
| **P.M.** | A1/A2 IM swim | [T] IM swim | A2 F/c & B/c swim | [T] F/c & B/c swim | | | |
| [SUBSET] | F/c Pull | Choice kick | Speed | IM kick | | | |
| Distance | 5.8 | 6.0 | 5.5 | 5.7 | | | |
| **LAND** | | Swiss Ball (pre swim) | | Med Ball (pre swim) | | General Circuit (post swim) | |
| **DAILY TOTAL** | 5.8 | 6.0 | 10.0 | 5.7 | 0.0 | 6.3 | DAY OFF |
| | | | | | | **WEEKLY TOTAL** | 33.8 |

(c) A Training to Train microcycle

| DAY DATE | MONDAY | TUESDAY | WEDNESDAY | THURSDAY | FRIDAY | SATURDAY | SUNDAY |
|---|---|---|---|---|---|---|---|
| **A.M.** | A1/A2 F/c & B/c swim | [T] No1 swim | | A1/A2 F/c-& B/c swim | La Tol No1 swim | A2/[T] IM/No1 swim | |
| [SUBSET] | No1 drills | A1 IM swim | | No1 kick | A1 recovery | A1 recovery | |
| Distance | 5.0 | | | | 5.0 | 7.0 | |
| **P.M.** | A2 IM swim | A1/A2 B/c swim | [T] IM swim | A2 IM swim | A1 recovery mixed swim/drills | | |
| [SUBSET] | No1 kick | F/c pull | A1 recovery | No1 pull | | | |
| Distance | 6.4 | 6.0 | 6.2 | 6.6 | 5.8 | | |
| **LAND** | | Power Circuit (pre swim) | Weights (am) | Med Ball (pre swim) | | General Circuit (post swim) | |
| DAILY TOTAL | 11.4 | 6.0 | 6.2 | 6.6 | 10.8 | 7.0 | DAY OFF |
| | | | | | | WEEKLY TOTAL | 48.0 |

(d) A Training to Compete microcycle

| DAY DATE | MONDAY | TUESDAY | WEDNESDAY | THURSDAY | FRIDAY | SATURDAY | SUNDAY |
|---|---|---|---|---|---|---|---|
| **A.M.** | A1/A2 (IM+F/c K/Pl/Sw) | A1/A2 (F/c+Choice sw) | | A2 (Choice K/Pl/Sw) | A1 Recovery (F/c overdistance Sw) | [T]/VO2 (IM/No1 sw) | |
| [SUBSET] | A1 (No1 tech) | Sp/Pwr (Choice sw) | | A1 (No1 Tech) | | A1 Recovery (Choice K/Dr/Sw) | |
| Distance | 6.0 | 6.0 | | 6.1 | 6.5 | 6.0 | |
| **P.M.** | A2/[T] (No1 kick) | [T] (No1 sw) | A2 (F/c+Form sw) | [T] (F/c+Form sw) | A2 (F/c+IM Pl) | | |
| [SUBSET] | A2 (F/c+Form Pl) | A2 (No1 Tech) | A2/[T] No1+Choice k) | A2 ·(F/c+Form Dr/Sw) | Sp/Pwr (No1 sw) | | |
| Distance | 6.3 | 6.4 | 6.5 | 7.0 | 6.2 | | |
| **LAND** | Specific Weights Flexibility | Circuits | Specific Weights Flexibility | Circuits | Specific Weights Flexibility | Circuits | |
| DAILY TOTAL | 12.3 | 12.4 | 6.5 | 13.1 | 12.7 | 6.0 | DAY OFF |
| | | | | | | WEEKLY TOTAL | 63.0 |

(e) A Training to Win microcycle

*Fig. 19 (a–e). Sample microcycles for LTAD framework.*

Fig. 19 (a–e) illustrates various planning models typical of a particular training phase for different ages of swimmers. Note that examples having two rows indicate both morning and afternoon sessions on that day. Definitions of the individual types of training may vary from coach to coach; those used in Fig. 19 are the training categories previously presented in *Crowood Sports Guides: Swimming.*

The discussion of training planning thus far has perhaps naturally focused mainly on the pool-training elements of a programme.

However, many other elements of training and education must be added to the coach's plan; these include programme areas such as strength and flexibility training, mental-skills training, self-management skills and so on. Some of these programme components may take place away from the pool environment and some will be constantly reinforced as part of regular coach–swimmer interaction. The coach must learn to plan every aspect of the programme so that nothing is excluded or neglected.

## Training Principles

### Individuality

Every individual is different and will respond to training in a unique way. This may seem obvious, but research conducted in the UK, by coach Ian Wright of Warrender BC in Edinburgh, has shown that most swimming programmes are conducted on a group or squad basis and that only the very highest-level performers have anything close to an individualized programme. There are many reasons for this (with lack of resources being the major reason cited), but nevertheless, acknowledging the individual response to training is a fundamental tenet of designing and implementing effective training programmes. For example, in designing a land-training programme for swimmers, coaches should consider: chronological age, training age, gender, event, distance and so on.

### Adaptation

Training has an effect on the human body; indeed the purpose of training is to have the desired effect on the body or, more specifically, its processes. This, or these, effect(s) are governed by the principle of adaptation. Placing the systems in the body under stress will produce responses associated with the type of training performed. For example, a common adaptation (inappropriate for swimming) to strength training is hypertrophy of muscle fibres. Unless the correct training is prescribed, this may result in swimmers becoming more muscle bound, heavier and slower in the water, quite the opposite from the original intention. Some training adaptations take place in a matter of days while others may take weeks or months. For effective training adaptations there must be: correct training; nutrients for growth and repair of tissues; and sufficient rest for the growth and repair to take place.

### Overload

Probably the most important principle of all – the concept of overload in training – is almost certainly the oldest of all principles. In order for adaptations to take place, the stress on the body's systems must be significant enough for physiological changes to occur, i.e. greater than 'usual'. The same stimuli will not provoke continued improvements and therefore the principle of overloading must be applied. There is a danger in overloading and it is the careful application of this principle that brings us to the next consideration.

### Progression

Often coupled with overload as a double-whammy principle, the use of a progressive or 'step-wise' approach to training prescription is the most obvious application of periodization in action. Too much loading at once could result in over-training or injury, and too little could result in no improvements being made. Swimming is a sport in which it is easy to see the principles of progressive overload being used, For example, longer distances, less rest, more repetitions, faster effort and so on. The systematic treatment of training programmes, in a structured and progressive manner, is the result of careful and considered planning by effective coaches. In terms of land training, the progressive-overload principle is also easily controlled with time, resistance and sets/reps being the most dominant variables.

### Specificity

Although another obvious principle, the use of specificity by swimming coaches is at times questionable. It is easy to note that regular running or cycling will not improve butterfly swimming performance, but research again shows that coaches are less than precise about their specific, individualized prescription of training. Coaches should consider the following four aspects when applying the principle of specificity: the event; the stroke; the target speed; and the energy-system demands of these combined. By considering these aspects alongside the individual characteristics of each swimmer, an appropriate and challenging land-based programme can be designed to complement the pool-based training plan.

### Variation

As far as skill learning is concerned, the greater the range of opportunities given to swimmers, the greater the likelihood that they will improve. In land training, this should mean that coaches are innovative and challenging with the range of exercises and options they prescribe; for example, can you devise an exercise that is more stroke-specific? The use of the variation principle can sometimes be overdone and care should be taken to use variety as a motivational tool rather than simply an end in its own right.

### Reversibility

Often simplified to 'if you do not use it, you lose it', this principle is more obvious after a period away from training, as swimmers discover how hard it is to gain fitness over a period of time, but how easy it is to lose it much more quickly. In terms of land training, this is often thought of as an issue in relation to strength gains made through weight training being lost when weight training is discontinued. If no other training is done to build on these gains, then obviously, they will be lost; but as long as 'conversion' training is done to apply the gains in the pool, the issue is less important.

### Balance

Associated with the principle of variation, this principle recognizes that you cannot do everything at once. Applying training principles successfully requires as much art as science, and the principle of balance is where the coach can be creative in the design and implementation of training. For example, determining how much and what types of land training to do is just as important as when and how much anaerobic training should be done in the pool.

### Long-Term Planning

'It takes ten years of extensive practice to excel in anything,' according to Nobel Laureate, H. A. Simon. This is never truer than in the field of training for sports performance. Translating the quote into the language of swimming training, this is three to four hours per day of deliberate practice for ten years and is supported by empirical and anecdotal evidence from successful swimmers. The British Swimming LTAD framework has already been outlined.

## PERIODIZATION OF LAND TRAINING

In order to best explain the process of periodizing land training for swimming it is probably most useful to use real examples. Fig. 20 shows the annual pattern of strength training loads for an élite swimmer preparing for Olympic-level competition.

Key features of this plan are the cyclical nature of the loading and unloading phases (particularly when competitions are undertaken) and the significant reduction of loads corresponding to the tapering periods. Looking at elements of the plan in more detail, Fig. 21 shows the first cycle of work (three weeks) after the Olympic trials.

Significant in this detailed plan is the fact that the loadings and depth of work are back to reasonably high levels. There will have been a significant detraining effect throughout the taper and it is important to regain conditioning and move on to new levels as soon as the body allows. Comparison of the volume loads (Fig. 22) from weeks 19 and 20 in Cycle 6 to those from earlier in the season, i.e. weeks 5 and 6 in Cycle 4, clearly shows this point.

Looking at a slightly different plan of sixteen weeks for another swimmer (Fig. 23), we can see that this was a very hard phase of work

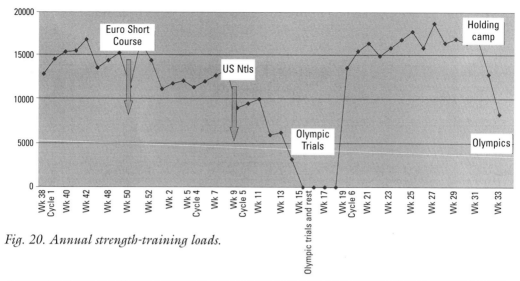

Fig. 20. *Annual strength-training loads.*

| | | Mon 3 May | | | | | Mon 10 May | | | | | Mon 17 May | | | | |
|---|---|---|---|---|---|---|---|---|---|---|---|---|---|---|---|---|
| | | **Wk 19** | | | | | **Wk 20** | | | | | **Wk 21** | | | | |
| | **Session 1** | | | | | | | | | | | | | | | |
| | **Exercises** | W-up | sets | reps | RI | TL | W-up | sets | reps | RI | TL | W-up | sets | reps | RI | TL |
| | BB warm-up | | | | | | | | | | | | | | | |
| 1 | Hang clean & jerk | 2x6 | 3 | 6 | l | 52 kg | 2x6 | 3 | 6 | mh | 62 kg | 2x6 | 3 | 6 | h | 65 kg |
| 2 | Back squat | | 3 | 8 | l | 72 kg | | 3 | 8 | m | 82 kg | | 3 | 8 | mh | 86 kg |
| 3 | CG SLDL | | 3 | 8 | l | 54 kg | | 3 | 8 | m | 61 kg | | 3 | 8 | mh | 65 kg |
| 4 | Bench press | | 3 | 8 | l | 44 kg | | 3 | 8 | m | 49 kg | | 3 | 8 | mh | 52 kg |
| 5 | Straight arm DB pullovers | | 3 | 8 | l | 15 kg | | 3 | 8 | m | 17 kg | | 3 | 8 | mh | 18 kg |
| 6 | Supine pull-ups | | 3 | | max | 0 kg | | 3 | | max | 0 kg | | 3 | | max | 0 kg |
| 7 | | | | | | 0 kg | | | | | 0 kg | | | | | 0 kg |
| | **Session 2** | | | | | | | | | | | | | | | |
| | **Exercises** | W-up | sets | reps | RI | TL | W-up | sets | reps | RI | TL | W-up | sets | reps | RI | TL |
| | BB warm-up | | | | | | | | | | | | | | | |
| 1 | Hang snatch (knee) | 3x6 | 3 | 6 | l | 40 kg | 3x6 | 3 | 6 | m | 46 kg | 3x6 | 3 | 6 | mh | 48 kg |
| 2 | Overhead squat | | 3 | 8 | l | 34 kg | | 3 | 8 | m | 38 kg | | 3 | 8 | mh | 40 kg |
| 3 | SG SLDL | | 3 | 8 | l | 42 kg | | 3 | 8 | m | 48 kg | | 3 | 8 | mh | 50 kg |
| 4 | SG shrugs | | 3 | 8 | l | 55 kg | | 3 | 8 | m | 62 kg | | 3 | 8 | mh | 66 kg |
| 5 | Bentover DB flyers | | 3 | 8 | l | 7 kg | | 3 | 8 | m | 8 kg | | 3 | 8 | mh | 9 kg |
| 6 | Chin-ups for speed | | 5 | 5 | | 0 kg | | 5 | 5 | | 0 kg | | 5 | 5 | | 0 kg |
| 7 | | | | | | 0 kg | | | | | 0 kg | | | | | 0 kg |
| | **Session 3** | | | | | | | | | | | | | | | |
| | **Exercises** | W-up | sets | reps | RI | TL | W-up | sets | reps | RI | TL | W-up | sets | reps | RI | TL |
| | BB warm-up | | | | | | | | | | | | | | | |
| 1 | Drop snatch | 2x6 | 3 | 6 | l | 36 kg | 2x6 | 3 | 6 | m | 40 kg | 2x6 | 3 | 6 | mh | 43 kg |
| 2 | Power clean | | 3 | 6 | l | 57 kg | | 3 | 6 | m | 65 kg | | 3 | 6 | mh | 69 kg |
| 3 | Front squat | | 3 | 8 | l | 54 kg | | 3 | 8 | m | 61 kg | | 3 | 8 | mh | 65 kg |
| 4 | Single leg DB SLDL | | 3 | 8 | l | 0 kg | | 3 | 8 | m | 0 kg | | 3 | 8 | mh | 0 kg |
| 5 | Bench press | | 3 | 8 | l | 44 kg | | 3 | 8 | m | 49 kg | | 3 | 8 | mh | 52 kg |
| 6 | Bentover DB flyers | | 3 | 8 | l | 7 kg | | 3 | 8 | m | 8 kg | | 3 | 8 | mh | 9 kg |
| 7 | Dips for speed | | 5 | 5 | | 0 kg | | 5 | 5 | | 0 kg | | 5 | 5 | | 0 kg |

Trunk strengthening exercises: do one from each group at the end of each session

| Russian twist | 4x10 | | Hanging leg raise | 4x10 |
|---|---|---|---|---|
| Candletsicks | 4x8 | | Suspended leg raise | 4x10 |
| Windscreen wiper | 4x10 | | Hanging windscreen wipers | 4x8 |
| BB rollouts | 4x10 | | Flat crunch | 4x10 |
| Plate walks | 4x10 m | | Reverse crunch | 4x10 |
| Weighted sit-ups | 4x10 | | Side bridge | 3x30:10 s |
| | | | Prone bridge | 4x30:10 s |

*Fig. 21. Training cycle 6.*

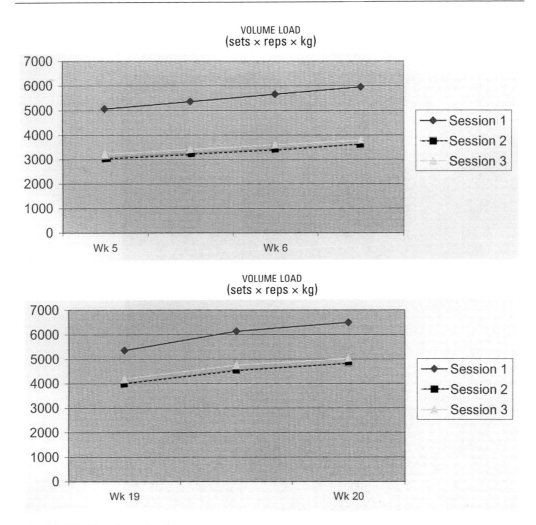

*Fig. 22. Weekly volume loads.*

(three weights sessions per week throughout), with there actually being a reduction in the amount of swimming done by this sprinter; the intention was to significantly increase strength over the period of the mesocycle and (ideally) convert this into power and speed gains in the pool later in the season. This is the classic dichotomy discussed earlier in the 'value' debate and there is no perfect answer apparent. The coach and swimmer in this example felt that it was for the greater good to adopt this strategy and certainly the fact that it was a sprint swimmer was probably a major factor in making this decision. However, if they had taken the 'new thinking' approach suggested earlier, it may have been more appropriate to target specific areas of strength that were deficient and detracting from performance rather than adopt a generalized strength-training programme, which this in effect was.

45

| Month | April | | | | May | | | | | | June | | | July | | | |
|---|---|---|---|---|---|---|---|---|---|---|---|---|---|---|---|---|---|
| Week number | 14 | 15 | 16 | 17 | 18 | 19 | 20 | 21 | 22 | 23 | 24 | 25 | 26 | 27 | 28 | 29 | 30 |
| Monday | 29 | 5 | 12 | 19 | 26 | 3 | 10 | 17 | 24 | 31 | 7 | 14 | 21 | 28 | 5 | 12 | 19 |
| Sunday | 4 | 11 | 18 | 25 | 2 | 9 | 16 | 23 | 30 | 6 | 13 | 20 | 27 | 4 | 11 | 18 | 25 |
| Competition | | | | | | | | | | | | | | | | | |
| Strength training | Cycle 5 | | | | Cycle 6 | | | | | | Cycle 7 | | | | | | |
| Phase | gpp | | | | spp | | | | | | spp | | | | | | |
| Frequency | 3 | 3 | 3 | 3 | 3 | 3 | 3 | 3 | 3 | 3 | 3 | 3 | 3 | 3 | 3 | 3 | |
| Intensity | l | ml | m | mh | ml | m | mh | h | m | vh | m | mh | h | mh | vh | h | |
| Exercises | Combination lifts, timed sets - Reps: 10>>8>>6 | | | | OL and strength exercises - Reps: 8>>6>>4>>2 | | | | | | OL and strength exercises - Reps: 8>>6>>4>>2 | | | | | | |
| Vibration | | | | | | | | | | | | | | | | | |
| Tests | Muscle lab | | | | Muscle lab | | | | | | Muscle lab | | | | | | |

*Fig. 23. A sprinter's mesocycle.*

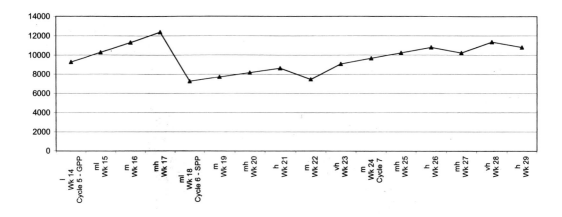

*Fig. 24. Training-load chart.*

The summary volume loading is shown in the training-load chart above (Fig. 24), and it indicates that a pretty high level of work was maintained throughout, with much less unloading than was apparent in the previous example.

What is clear from these examples is that a high degree of planning and systematic process is applied to the periodization of land training within the overall plan of élite swimmers with access to specialist support. There are varying degrees of success with this and

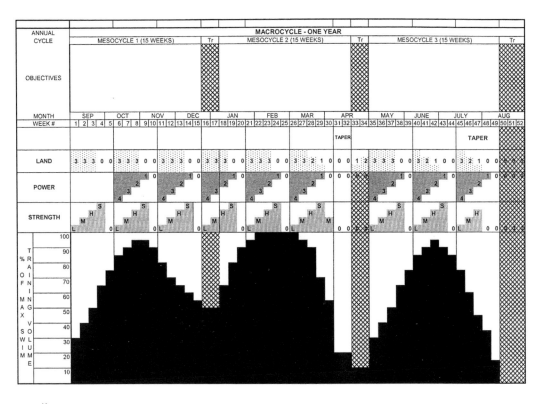

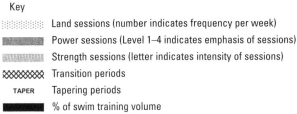

**Key**

| | |
|---|---|
| ░░░░░░ | Land sessions (number indicates frequency per week) |
| ▓▓▓▓ | Power sessions (Level 1–4 indicates emphasis of sessions) |
| ▒▒▒▒ | Strength sessions (letter indicates intensity of sessions) |
| ✕✕✕✕✕ | Transition periods |
| TAPER | Tapering periods |
| ███ | % of swim training volume |

*Fig. 25. AIP seasonal plan.*

several anecdotal accounts tell of effective planning between swimming coaches and strength and conditioning coaches, alongside much gnashing of teeth as both sides attempt to stand their ground. What is needed is consideration of the swimmer's body as one organism to be trained, conditioned and honed to perfection by each training mode complementing the other. What follows is an attempt to explain this course of action.

## Asynchronous Integrated Periodization (AIP) of Land Training for Swimming

The practical application of this section has not been experimentally tested and represents

| DAY DATE | MONDAY | TUESDAY | WEDNESDAY | THURSDAY | FRIDAY | SATURDAY | SUNDAY |
|---|---|---|---|---|---|---|---|
| **A.M.** | A1 (Fc Swim overdistance) | A2 (Fc/Form/Fc - Pull) | | A1 Recovery (Bk Pull + Swim) | | VO2 (No1 swim) | |
| [SUBSET] | A1 (I.M. Technique) | Sp/Pwr (Choice Swim + paddles) | | A1 (No.1 Skills) | | A2 (K/Pl/Sw - Choice) | |
| Distance | 6.2 | 5.3 | | 6.5 | | 6.5 | |
| **P.M.** | A2 (Swim - Fc + Fly) | [T] (Swim - Fc + Form) | A2 (I.M. Swim overdistance) | [T] (Fc Swim) | A2 (Fc Pull - Hypoxic) | | |
| [SUBSET] | A2 (Fc Kick) | A1 (Technique - Fly + Fc) | A2 (Fc Kick) | A1 (Technique - Bk + Brst) | Sp/Pwr (Basic Speed - Choice) | | |
| Distance | 6.8 | 6.0 | 6.8 | 7.0 | 5.9 | | |
| Core | | | | | | | |
| Land | | Circuit A | | Circuit A | | Circuit C | |
| Power | Power 2 | | | | | | |
| Strength | | | Weights H | | Weights H | | |
| DAILY TOTAL (Swim volume) | 13.0 | 11.3 | 6.8 | 13.5 | 5.9 | 6.5 | DAY OFF |

WEEKLY TOTAL | 57.0

*Fig. 26. AIP microcycle.*

my interpretation of the theoretical principles based on several years experience as an élite swimming coach and coach educator. There are some elements of AIP present in the coaching process of some élite swimming coaches and this is not just another 'academic theory', but it is certainly not commonplace.

The following notes are given in explanation of the illustrated plans shown in Fig. 25, the annual plan, and Fig. 26, an example of a microcycle from the plan. The plan is a generic one and has not been fully adapted for swimmers of a specific stroke or event. For the purposes of interpreting the information, it is assumed that the details given apply to a 200m-swimmer.

The term Asynchronous Integrated Periodization (AIP) requires some explanation before examining the plan in more detail. 'Asynchronous' literally means 'out of step', and in this instance refers to the fact that not all aspects of training are progressing and overloading at the same time or the same rate, e.g. high volumes in the pool do not necessarily correspond with heavy resistance training, etc.,

although there are times when this may occur. 'Integrated' means included or incorporated, and this is the missing link in most cases. The fact that land training is part of the overall thinking process in annual planning is uncommon in many cases. 'Periodization' has been well explained elsewhere in this section of the book. Without being too pedantic about attaching other words to the term, AIP simply means 'systematic, out of step but incorporated, training plans'.

## Macrocycle

The annual plan shown in Fig. 25 shows one complete macrocycle and is typical of the current pattern in British swimming, which in turn reflects the international competition calendar. The actual competition outlets have not been illustrated other than to indicate when tapering periods occur, but they would probably be:

• A 'swim tired' but no real rest, taper or shave meet in December (could be European short course or a domestic event);

- Trials/GB championships meet in April;
- Major games/championship meet in the summer.

There would be other competitions throughout the season designed to meet individual needs for racing practice objectives, but, to amplify the main points about integrating the land and pool programmes, these have been omitted.

The basic pattern for the season is a three times 15-week mesocycle with transition/rest periods between. Other than the last three weeks, i.e. after the major summer competition, these periods are not complete rest, with some training objectives still to be met. For example, after the first mesocycle, the volume of pool training is around 50 per cent of the maximum to allow quality power, strength and landwork to occur. It also coincides with the festive holiday period and takes into account some of the 'domestic' constraints apparent at this time. Of course, if swimmers were abroad on warm-weather training camps, this situation would change, but the training objectives should basically remain the same. The second transition phase has only some land training and a maximum of four pool sessions for maintenance of fitness.

There is a school of thought that you should get swimmers back into the pool and full-time training again straight after a meet like this to negate any detraining effects, and I have witnessed the method proposed here and the opposite view – giving them a week off. On balance, the reasons for the approach in this plan are more psychological than physical, with mental as much as physical fatigue a recognized factor. This short phase (ten to fourteen days) is also a time for re-focusing on the major goals ahead. There will be some training done each day, so it is not a period of complete rest, but clearly some coaches will take a different view.

### Mesocycles (3 × 15 Weeks)

The full details of these component parts is not necessary here, but each mesocycle will include an emphasis, to a greater or lesser degree, on the following:

- Aerobic capacity (pool);
- Anaerobic power (pool);
- Stroke mechanics (pool);
- Optimum stroke rate and length (pool);
- Strength development (land);
- Power development (land);
- Flexibility development (land);
- General conditioning and co-ordination (land);
- Power development (pool);
- Racing skills (pool);
- Pacing and strategy (pool);
- Psychological skills, nutrition and life-style management.

The objectives for each mesocycle would be matched to the individual characteristics, specific event demands and needs of the swimmer, ensuring an individualized approach within a periodized framework. A tabulated representation of the AIP in Fig. 25 is shown in Fig. 27 with specific details of the land, power and strength sessions in the plan. The distinction between these training methods is not common in the planning of many coaches. 'Land' sessions in the form of circuit training are common methods of training, but the detail of different types of circuit sessions are a key feature of this plan. Additionally, 'power' sessions on land (and in the pool) are the bridging components of the AIP, attempting to 're-assign' the land-training gains into improved swimming performance. This is the weakest area in terms of research evidence to the contrary, but anecdotally swimmers report feelings of being stronger in the water or more powerful, and something must occur physiologically to ensure this happens. Strength sessions are also

49

| | Land sessions (number indicates frequency per week) |
|---|---|
| | Usually in the form of circuit training. There are three types: |
| | Circuit A – muscular endurance and aerobic activity; |
| | Circuit B – muscular endurance; |
| | Circuit B – recovery and flexibility. |
| | Power sessions (Level 1–4 indicates emphasis of sessions) |
| | There are four levels: |
| | Level 1 – stretchcords |
| | Level 2 – plyometric jumping and medicine balls |
| | Level 3 – swimbench |
| | Level 4 – sprint assisted and resisted swimming (in pool!) |
| | Strength sessions (letter indicates inttensity of sessions) |
| | Usually in the form of weight training. There are four lifting loads: |
| | Light load – speed of exercise is emphasized; stroke specific reps |
| | Medium load – high reps (12–20), strength-endurance |
| | High load – short reps (6–12), mainly upper body, strength power |
| | Super-high load – short reps (2–5), stroke specific exercises, max power |
| | Transition periods |
| | The periods between mesocycles, sometimes complete rest and regeneration (between macrocycles/seasons) and often an opportunity to emphasize particular training objectives (see below) |
| TAPER | Tapering periods |
| | The final preparatory phase leading up to major competitions. Individually focused, but usually planned to last anything from two to six weeks. |
| | % of swim training volume |
| | This is a very basic representation of another vital component of training. Shown here to illustrate the key stages in the AIP plan, the detailed balance of pool training requires further explanation than is given here. An exemplar microcycle is provided. |
| | Key stages exemplar |
| | An example of a key stage microcycle is shown in Fig. 26 with some detail of the AIP issues presented. |

Fig. 27. AIP key stages exemplar.

common, but the classification and sequencing of sessions is key to the effectiveness of the plan, as are the 'unloading' weeks when no strength sessions are performed.

### Key Stages (Fig. 27)

Using the analogy of the *Tour de France* cycle race, there are several 'key stages' in an annual training plan. Without delving into this analogy too deeply, the key stages referred to here might be analogous with the mountain stages of '*Le Tour*': not just one peak to be climbed, but a series of uphill, downhill and flat routes to be negotiated, having cycled a number of days previously and with a number of days still to follow before the end – much like a microcycle of training with its place in the overall seasonal plan and its challenges of balancing physiological, psychological and technical priorities on land and in the pool.

In the AIP seasonal plan shown in Fig. 25, one such key stage is taken from the first mesocycle. The example chosen (week 8) has all aspects of training contained within the week and is one of two 'high-volume' peaks in this phase of training.

### Example Microcycle (One Week)

To further reinforce the point about integrating the pool and land training, an example of a microcycle is shown in Fig. 26. This is one of the key stages in the seasonal plan where many aspects of training have potentially conflicting demands on the swimmer and careful balancing and scheduling of training is necessary. Taken in isolation it is relatively easy to plan a week's training, but as part of the integrated whole, there are many other factors to consider, particularly when, what and how often training should occur.

A lengthy discussion could take place on each and every aspect of this exemplar, including the pool-session pattern and emphasis, but the critical AIP points to be made are:

- The power 2 session is done at the start of the week to 'capture' the swimmers at their 'freshest' and gain maximal neurological and physiological benefits. A power 2 workout would include plyometric jumps and upper-body exercises with medium-heavy medicine balls, and could be done indoors or outdoors with space to move and weather the only considerations.

- Circuits are done for land training before Tuesday and Thursday evening pool sessions and after the Saturday morning session. With the emphasis on muscular endurance and general aerobic capacity, the midweek circuit A-type sessions simply add to the training stimulus, which is designed as aerobic in nature anyway. Saturday morning's circuit C-type session is more of a recovery-based session with an emphasis on flexibility and on quality of movement rather than on high-intensity exercise.

- Strength sessions are done on Wednesday and Friday mornings (just before lunchtime to allow for an afternoon rest period). In this example training week they are high-load sessions and the focus would be on individualized event-specific programmes for the upper body. The group may all train at the same time but, other than 'spotting' exercises for each other, they would not necessarily have to work together at all.

- The final general point in this and most other weeks is that core-stability training is a daily routine and not periodized on a physiological basis. Swimmers at this level would be expected to have their own Swiss balls and foam pieces to do their personal work, as prescribed by the team physiotherapist. During tapering periods this work would be reduced to suit each swimmer's needs as previously discussed.

| Name | | | | | | | | HEALTH / TRAINING STATUS | | | |
| --- | --- | --- | --- | --- | --- | --- | --- | --- | --- | --- | --- |
| | | | | | | | | Questionaire | | | |
| | | | Resting Heart rate | Sleep Quality | Sleep Length | Willingness to train | Mood state | Fatigue | Muscle Soreness | Recovery | Ener |
| Week Number | Mezocycle Name | Date | BPM | 1 to 5 | Hours | 1 to 5 | 1 to 5 | 1 to 5 | 1 to 5 | 1 to 5 | 1 to |
| | | | | | | | | | | | |
| | | | | | | | | | | | |
| | | | | | | | | | | | |
| | | | | | | | | | | | |
| | | | | | | | | | | | |
| | | | | | | | | | | | |
| | | | | | | | | | | | |
| | | | | | | | | | | | |
| | | | | | | | | | | | |
| | | | | | | | | | | | |
| | | | | | | | | | | | |
| | | | | | | | | | | | |
| | | | | | | | | | | | |
| | | | | | | | | | | | |
| | | | | | | | | | | | |
| | | | | | | | | | | | |
| | | | | | | | | | | | |
| | | | | | | | | | | | |
| | | | | | | | | | | | |
| | | | | | | | | | | | |
| | | | | | | | | | | | |
| | | | | | | | | | | | |
| | | | | | | | | | | | |

A final general point about this proposal is that it makes many assumptions about operating in a fairly 'constraint-free' environment. This may not be the case for every programme, but compromising on this type of 'ideal-model' would be pointless. Most of the recommendations in this proposal are achievable by the majority of programmes with an effective management of the process by the coach. Certainly there are no excuses for a lack of systematic planning and, if dedicated facilities or equipment are not available, then alternatives should be found. It is my fervent belief that asynchronous integrated periodization is within the control and capabilities of most swimming coaches. In fact, if you could 'download' the mind of an elite coach, you find it in there!

## Training Log

A training log is a tool that can help improve swimming performance. If used properly and accurately it may make training more effective in helping you understand yourself and how your body responds to training. This training log (Fig. 28) is designed to assist swimmers and coaches in tracking changes in certain parameters over time. The monitoring of these variables is very important in providing feedback. This feedback may be used to adapt current and future training, as well as to monitor seasonal changes in these parameters. It should be completed on a daily basis, in order to accurately reflect how the swimmer's body is responding to training. To receive the most benefit from your training log, it should be used on a con-

| | | | | TRAINING | | | | |
| | | | | Swimming | | | Dryland | |
| rition | Illness | Injury | Menstrual Cycle | Distance | Intensity | Total Time | Intensity | Total Time |
|---|---|---|---|---|---|---|---|---|
| to 5 | Y or N | Y or N | S or F | km | 1 to 5 | Min | 1 to 5 | Min |
| | | | | | | | | |
| | | | | | | | | |
| | | | | | | | | |
| | | | | | | | | |
| | | | | | | | | |
| | | | | | | | | |
| | | | | | | | | |
| | | | | | | | | |
| | | | | | | | | |
| | | | | | | | | |
| | | | | | | | | |
| | | | | | | | | |
| | | | | | | | | |
| | | | | | | | | |
| | | | | | | | | |
| | | | | | | | | |
| | | | | | | | | |
| | | | | | | | | |
| | | | | | | | | |
| | | | | | | | | |
| | | | | | | | | |
| | | | | | | | | |
| | | | | | | | | |

*Fig. 28. A training log.*

sistent and continuous basis. Initial use of the training log may take up to ten minutes a day. However, after becoming accustomed to the training log, you should be able to complete the log in no more than five minutes.

Below is a description of each item on the training log, along with the time of the day, morning (am) or afternoon (pm), that the item should be evaluated:

- Resting heart rate (am). Record your resting heart rate first thing in the morning while you are still lying in a prone position (flat) in bed. Heart rate can be taken either on the neck or the wrist. Your heart rate should be counted for exactly one minute beginning with zero, 1, 2, 3 and so on.

- Quality of sleep (am). Record how well you slept the previous night based on a five-point scale ranging from 'very poor' to 'very restful'.
- Length of sleep (am). Record how long you slept in hours. This should include only those hours of actual sleep from the previous night (not reading in bed, watching TV and so on).
- Willingness to train (am). Record your willingness to train based on a four-point scale ranging from 'did not train' to 'very willing'. Willingness to train relates directly to your training sessions that day.
- Mood state (am). Record your mood state on a five-point scale ranging from 'very un-motivated' to 'very motivated'. Mood state

is a reflection of how you feel (your state of mind) on that day and your motivation.

- Rating of fatigue (am). Record your fatigue level on a five-point scale ranging from 'high' to 'low'. Fatigue can be described as a feeling of excessive whole-body tiredness and exhaustion that affects the ability to function normally due to lack of energy. Usually, sleep will not relieve the feelings of fatigue. Fatigue is a long-term or extended feeling of heaviness and exhaustion that can be cumulative over time.

- Rating of muscle soreness (am). Record the rating of how sore your muscles are on a five -point scale ranging from 'severe pain' to 'no pain'. Muscle soreness is different from feeling discomfort from an injury. Muscle soreness is pain, discomfort or tenderness in muscles that results from regular swim and dryland training.

- Ability to recover (am). Record the rating of how well you can physically recover and recuperate after challenging sets and sessions based on a five-point scale ranging from 'very poor' to 'very good'.

- Energy levels (am). Related to willingness to train, how much energy do you feel you have for the day ahead?

- Nutrition (am). How well did you eat and re-hydrate? Clearly related to energy levels. Are your food stores replenished?

- How much was your training yesterday affected by illness? (am). Record how much an illness affected your training on a five-point scale ranging from 'could not swim' to 'not affected'.

- Was your training yesterday affected by pain or an injury? (am). Record whether or not your training was affected by an injury (yes or no).

- Start/finish of menstrual cycle. Record the day your menstrual cycle starts (S) and finishes (F) by placing the respective letter in the box.

- Total swimming volume (am and pm). Record actual total swimming distance for each session (in km). Morning and afternoon volumes should be recorded separately.

- Swimming intensity (am and pm). Record on the five-point scale how 'hard' the session was.

- Total dryland minutes. Record total minutes spent doing dryland exercises, including weights, med balls, cords, abs and so on.

- Dryland intensity (am and pm). Record on the five-point scale how 'hard' the session was.

- The session (am and pm). Record the detail of each set in each session.

Comments on main set (am and pm). Record any thoughts you have on your performance in the main set (how you felt, what you did or did not do well, and so on).

# CHAPTER 3

# Training

## WARMING UP

A common feature of modern land-based training is the concept of 'dynamic warm-ups'. More in keeping with the traditional practice of ballistic stretching, this 'new' mode of exercising has actually been around for decades and was an integral part of the Eastern Bloc's track and field programmes for many years. Coaches and swimmers may have some questions about this type of exercise and the following exchange should answer those most frequently asked:

### Dynamic Warm-Up (DWU)

Q: What is a dynamic warm-up?

A: A dynamic warm-up is essentially stretching with movement, and it represents a relatively new way of thinking about preparing your body to train. A dynamic warm-up typically involves performing exercises like arm swings, lunges and trunk twists – exercises that warm the body up and get the muscles working. This has been shown to be a very effective way for preparing the body to train in the pool and on dry land.

Q: What does a dynamic warm-up do for the body?

A: A dynamic warm-up does five very important things for a swimmer:

1. It increases body temperature. At slightly elevated temperatures muscles are able to contract more efficiently and generate greater force.

2. It primes the cardiovascular system and gets the heart and lungs ready to engage in vigorous activity. This helps to deliver oxygen to working muscles more efficiently.

3. It elongates muscles actively. This improves joint range of motion as well as the body's ability to handle the forces experienced during training and competition.

4. It helps to establish proper movement patterns for training and competition.

---

### Exercise Prescription Key

The exercises and routines in this section of the book are coded according to the LTAD model. If it is not explicitly stated in the text, a suffix code will be attached to the exercise description. These codes are:

**FUN** – FUNdamentals: movement literacy.
**SwSk** – SwimSkills: building technique.
**T2T** – Training to Train: building the engine.
**T2C** – Training to Compete: optimizing the engine.
**T2W** – Training to Win: top performance.

**This means that the exercise(s) is(are) best suited to this stage of development. Care should be taken to avoid doing exercises at an inappropriate level above that stated, but of course all exercises at the stage below can be done at any time.**

---

5. The dynamic warm-up 'wakes up' the nervous system and gets the brain communicating effectively with the muscles, allowing your muscles to work more efficiently.

Q: Should not a warm-up include static stretching?

A: If you are like most people, when you hear the words 'warm-up' you think of a pre-practice or pre-competition routine that contains static stretching – the type of stretching where you put a muscle under light tension and then hold that position for 15–30 seconds. However, recent research has shown that static stretching may not be appropriate when preparing to train or swim in a race because it can reduce the amount of force and power the stretched muscles can generate. These effects can last for more than one hour after stretching. Therefore it is recommended that a dynamic warm-up – in place of static stretching – be performed before every session or competition. Remember that your normal warm-up in the pool is basically a form of DWU in itself, if performed correctly.

Q: Does that mean that static stretching is bad for you?

A: Static stretching is still very important for swimmers, since it helps to improve flexibility and joint range of motion – the issue is more about when it should be performed. Regular static stretching should still be a part of every swimmer's training programme. However, it should be performed after training or racing, during a cool-down period – as part of recovery – and not as part of a warm-up routine.

Q: Are there any other guidelines for performing a dynamic warm-up?

A: There are. Some things to think about include:

• Each dynamic warm-up routine should follow 3–5 minutes of a light general warm-up activity, something like jogging, riding a stationary bike, or skipping.
• You do not need to rest for long periods of time between exercises; 15–30 seconds of rest should be enough to recover for the next exercise.
• Dynamic warm-up exercises do not need to be performed on poolside. You can use a gym, a field, a tennis court or anywhere you have enough space to perform the exercises safely.

Q: Where can I get more information on dynamic warm-ups?

A: Read on! An example of a dynamic warm-up routine that I use with swimmers is shown in Figs 29–40.

## The DWU

*Walk and Lunge  (Fig. 29)*
Step forward and walk across the room gradually getting lower and lower on the movement. The aim is to perform almost a full, one-legged squat by the end of a 25m distance (repeat on way back).

---

**Top Tip**
Always maintain your posture with tight abdominals/trunk.

---

*Standing Squat  (Fig. 30)*
In the same starting position, perform a standing squat progressively getting lower and lower on each exercise (two sets of ten).

*Forward Hamstring Kick (Each Leg) (Fig. 31)*
Keeping the kicking leg straight, gradually build up a forward kicking and backward swinging motion. Let the leg swing all the

*Fig. 29. Walk and lunge.*

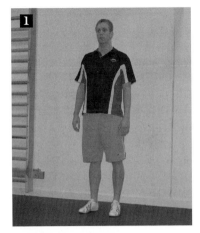 

*Fig. 30. Standing squat.*

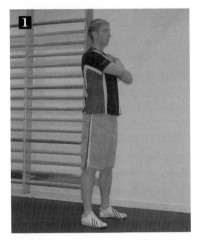 

*Fig. 31. Forward hamstring kick.*

*Fig. 32. Grapevine walk.*

*Fig. 33. Lunges.*

Fig. 34. Sideways hamstring kick.

Fig. 35. High knee walk.

way back naturally and keep the heel down and toes up on the forward action (two sets of 15 with each leg).

*Grapevine Walk (Both Directions) (Fig. 32)*
Using the dance/aerobic class movement known as a grapevine step, get gradually lower each time as you cross the room, then repeat with the other leg crossing behind. This is a clumsy looking movement if done poorly, but very good for posture and control when performed well.

*Lunges (Forward, 45 Degrees, Sideways) (Fig. 33)*
Similar to the walk and lunge at the start (*see* Fig. 29), stay in a static position and perform ten progressively lower forward lunges: ten at a 45-degree diagonal and ten directly out to the side. Alternate legs for each position.

*Sideways Hamstring Kick (Fig. 34)*
As with the forward hamstring kick (*see* Fig. 31, but without crossing the mid-point on the way back. Perform sideways straight leg kicks progressively higher (one set of ten on each leg).

*High Knee Walk (Fig. 35)*
Over a similar distance to the walk and lunge, perform a progressively higher knee lift each step (use your arms to generate height), repeat on the way back.

*Quad Stretch (Donkey Kick) (Fig. 36)*
In a three-point stance, perform progressively higher backwards donkey kicks leading with the heel (ten with each leg).

*Chest Flies/Back Slap (Fig. 37)*
A bit like old-fashioned chest expanders, alternately swing the arms out at shoulder

*Fig. 36. Quad stretch (donkey kick).*

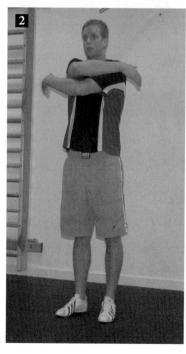

*Fig. 37. Chest flies/back slap.*

*Fig. 38. Backward lunge (calf stretch).*

height to stretch the chest and shoulders and hug the back (15 in total).

*Backward Lunge (Calf Stretch) (Fig. 38)*
Standing upright, step back with each leg alternately and press the heel down, stretching the calf and Achilles tendon. Be careful with this to begin with: gradually increase the movement over ten repetitions per leg.

*Alternate Arms Press Back (Fig. 39)*
Start with one arm above the head and one by the side and alternately swing them up/back and down/back, increasing the range as the exercise progresses (20 in total).

*Keyholes (Fig. 40)*
Stand in a 'praying' position, then push your hands apart, then lift above your head and clap them together vigorously behind the back.

*Fig. 39. Alternate arms press back.*

 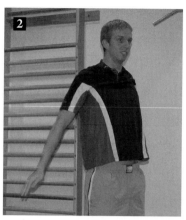

*Fig. 40. Keyholes.*

In total, this routine can be performed in 15–20 minutes at the start of a land-training session throughout the season. Coaches can use some or all of the exercises, but be sure to cover all muscles to be exercised in the session to follow and ensure that each exercise and the whole routine is performed progressively. In terms of the LTAD model, this routine can be done by all swimmers, although at the early stages, it is much more about learning how to perform the exercises (one per week maybe) than actually receiving any physiological benefit from them. Simply being able to control the entire body in some of these movements will be a challenge to younger swimmers.

A quick reference musculature chart is provided in Fig. 41 (a) and (b). Coaches should be familiar with the main muscle groups involved in competitive swimming and the exercises that can be used to improve conditioning.

The remainder of this part of the book is dedicated to outlining different forms of exercise and, with the aid of photographs, explaining how they should be done. First, pre-swim preparation is considered in terms of injury prevention and warm-up, then the important area of circuit training is introduced. Two significant sections on Swiss-ball and medicine-ball training follow. Swim-bench training and stretchcords are then covered followed by resistance training. A short section detailing with simple, home-based exercises is presented, and then the final section covers stretching and flexibility training, particularly as a means of recovery.

## PRE-SWIM PREPARATION

Swimming being the demanding and rigorous sport that it is results in it being fairly common for children to start training at a young age. In a typical 2-hour pool session, an élite-level competitive swimmer may swim upwards of 6,000m (long course). This amounts to covering an average of 40-plus miles per week, which is the land equivalent of running more than 100 miles (not uncommon for Paula Radcliff, but certainly not the norm). This high volume (yardage in coaching parlance) means that competitive swimmers perform somewhere between 2,000 and 4,000 stroke cycles per day, or well in excess of 1,000,000 stroke cycles per year. Since female swimmers, on average, have shorter arm strokes, they may perform an additional 660,000 stroke cycles per year! Thus, it should be no surprise that shoulder pain is one of the leading ailments among competitive swimmers.

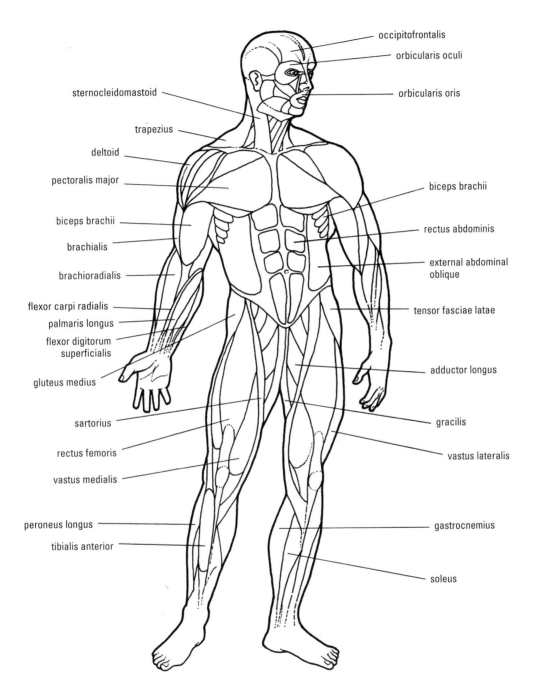

occipitofrontalis

orbicularis oculi

sternocleidomastoid

orbicularis oris

trapezius

deltoid

pectoralis major

biceps brachii

biceps brachii

rectus abdominis

brachialis

external abdominal oblique

brachioradialis

flexor carpi radialis

tensor fasciae latae

palmaris longus

flexor digitorum superficialis

gluteus medius

adductor longus

sartorius

gracilis

rectus femoris

vastus lateralis

vastus medialis

peroneus longus

gastrocnemius

tibialis anterior

soleus

*Fig. 41 (a). Musculature chart (front).*

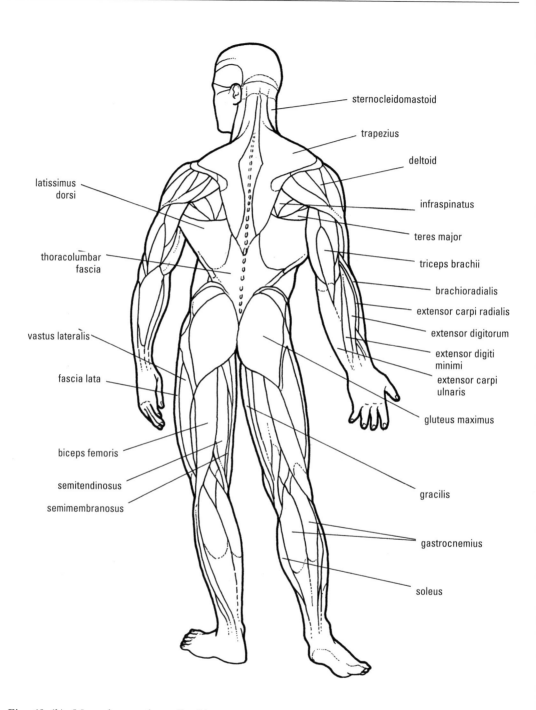

*Fig. 41 (b). Musculature chart (back).*

The causes of shoulder pain are complex and may include the athlete's gender, stroke technique, training age, training distance, stroke choice, training intensity, land-training programme, use of hand paddles and so on. A survey in the United States demonstrated that more than a third of senior national and Olympic swimmers experienced shoulder pain that prevented them from training effectively.

Since the term 'swimmer's shoulder' was first coined in the 1970s, many researchers have sought to discover the cause of shoulder pain in swimmers. The current understanding is that swimming selectively strengthens the anterior chest muscles and internal rotators of the shoulder and, when combined with repetitive strain to the shoulder, fosters an imbalance in the dynamic stability of the shoulder joint. Studies have found that this abnormal internal-to-external rotator torque ratio is an unavoidable consequence of swimming and is present from age-group to senior level.

The terms laxity and instability are commonly used when referring to joints, but there is a significant difference between the two. Laxity refers to the normal, painless freedom of movement around a joint, while instability refers to the tendency of a joint to subluxate or dislocate, resulting in pain or functional impairment. Asymptomatic, increased range of motion (ROM) or laxity, of the shoulder can be found in a large proportion of swimmers, especially those at the élite competitive level. Significant controversy surrounds whether swimmers acquire shoulder laxity as a result of repetitive motion of swimming, or whether swimmers with inherent shoulder laxity are more efficient in the water, which leads them to stay in the sport longer and compete at a higher level. Regardless of its origin, shoulder (glenohumeral) laxity is facilitated by the repetitive overuse and muscular imbalances associated with swimming. This laxity may lead to instability and secondary impingement, causing shoulder pain.

> **Important!**
> Training programmes should be monitored to minimize the risk of injury.

Similar to athletes in other competitive sports, most swimmers conduct a stretching routine prior to exercise. Unfortunately, stretching may be more harmful than helpful. For example, most of the stretches that swimmers perform, including partner stretches, serve to stretch the anterior capsule of the shoulder. If the capsule is over-stretched, the risk of instability and subsequent injury permanently increases. Therefore, the need for pre-swim static stretching in swimming is limited. Any stretching should be specific to the individual, prescribed by a physiotherapist and designed to correct specific muscular or capsular tightness. Fig. 42 (*see* page 66) shows examples of stretching exercises to be avoided. The flexibility exercises in the last part of this section of the book details the way in which swimmers should use stretching as part of their normal routine.

A much more effective pre-swimming ritual should be the use of stretchcords, surgical tubing or 'therapeutic bands'. Relatively inexpensive and easy to modify, these can be an invaluable tool to swimmers and coaches in preventing injury and strengthening the shoulder. The exercises are simple to do and easy to organize. Fig. 43 (a) shows the movement of internal rotation; attach the band just above waist height to a suitable point (in this case the backstroke flags), keep the elbow fixed and by the side, then bring your hand in towards the body for three sets of ten with 30 seconds rest. External rotation involves the same fixed position for the band and elbow but facing the other way (or using the opposite hand), move the hand outwards – *see* Fig. 43 (b). There are many other band exercises that can be done as part of a land-training

*Fig. 42. Pre-swim stretches to be avoided.*

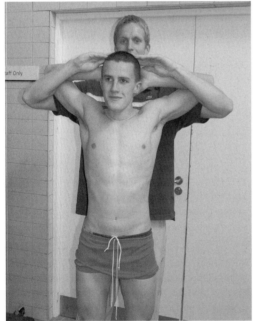

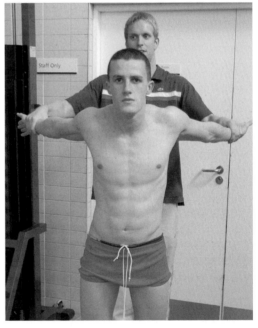

programme and these are outlined later in the relevant part of this section. The availability of different thicknesses of tubing/bands mean that these simple but effective preventative exercises can be (and should be) done by all swimmers from SwimSkills onwards, i.e. once they are making a commitment to some regular form of 'training'. It is interesting to note that these same exercises shown in Fig. 43 form part of the development programme for junior tennis players in North America, as the US Tennis Association

*Fig. 43 (a). Pre-swim
internal rotation
exercises.*

*Fig. 43 (b). Pre-swim external rotation exercises.*

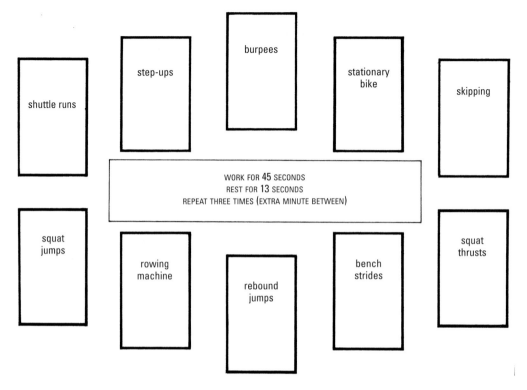

*Fig. 44. An aerobic circuit.*

(USTA) attempts to curb overuse injury problems in younger players.

## CIRCUIT TRAINING

Circuit training (more commonly called 'circuits') is a comparatively new addition in the field of physical training, making its first appearance in the mid-1950s, with new commercial varieties, such as boxercise and body pump, coming on the health and fitness club scene every year. The aim of circuit training is a progressive development of the muscular and respiratory systems of the body. Throughout this type of training, participants are usually treated as individuals and not as a group, pushing themselves to their own limits with minimum intervention from the coach. Circuits are frequently mentioned in the early dryland texts by Counsilman, Dawson and Hogg, as discussed in Chapter 1.

Circuit training is usually designed to improve all-round physical fitness rather than fitness for a specific sport. Thus, it is normally part of pre- or early-season training programmes in swimming. However, 'swim-specific' circuits can easily be implemented into your sessions. You can design circuits to improve any of the main physical components of fitness: strength, speed, endurance, flexibility, power, speed, and so on. But it should be recognized that muscular and respiratory systems can be improved only through carefully planned and well-executed training pro-grammes. Key considerations when planning a circuit session are:

- The standard of fitness;
- Numbers of swimmers involved;
- What the objective of the circuit is;
- Amount of time available;
- Space and equipment that is available;
- Motivational music and a suitable sound system;
- Clear, easy-to-follow circuit cards/instruc-tions.

Exercises (sometimes called 'stations') must be selected and arranged so that all appropri-ate factors of fitness and the overload princi-ple are considered. Circuit training is unlike weight training, where the athlete usually works at, or near, a maximum-weight level with the weight that they can successfully han-dle for a definite number of repetitions, and then has a period of rest before making repeated attempts at the exercise. The princi-ple of circuit training is that the swimmer works at sub-maximum level over an extend-ed period of time with either no rest, or min-imal rest, between exercises. The whole musculature of the body should be exercised and no one muscle group should be exercised consecutively; and throughout the circuit, the exercises should be varied enough to cover the full range of movement for that particular group. The overall aim and stage of the season should be reflected in the type of circuit – e.g. endurance at the start of the season – and in the number/duration of rest and repetitions.

In general, the circuit should follow a logi-cal sequence with an easy to follow plan. (Fig. 44 shows an aerobic-type circuit that can be done by swimmers from SwSk➤T2W.) This becomes more apparent especially when the circuit becomes more complicated in its make-up. Careful planning and preparation,

knowing in advance the limitations on time, group size and available equipment, will all help in your setting up of the circuit. The con-trolling factor of the circuit also needs time spent on it in the planning stage. This can be done in a couple of ways such as:

- The coach – with whistle – stops and starts each exercise for a prescribed number of seconds, e.g. 45 seconds on and 15 seconds off. If music is available, this is also an excellent cue to rest/work.
- A specific number of repetitions per exercise, then move on with no extra rest. This is fine with lots of space and smaller groups, but can generate 'queuing' in tight spaces with large groups.

The success of a circuit will depend on the coach's personality and the swimmers' motiva-tion. Correct performance of exercises must be insisted on: if cheating methods are allowed, the benefits gained will be reduced consider-ably. Safety for the swimmer and mainte-nance/repair of equipment must always be considered when devising a circuit, especially when improvising and where unusual appara-tus is being used. Check all equipment prior to beginning each session, i.e. benches are firm, stretchcords are secure and so on.

Other types of circuit to the common ones mentioned above are listed below.

*Pairs (SwSk➤ T2W)*
Swimmers are paired off with a partner of similar capabilities and motivation. The appa-ratus to be worked on is also duplicated. Each swimmer competes simultaneously against the other in the number of repetitions at-tained in the preset time.

*Triples (SwSk➤ T2W)*
Apparatus laid in triplicate – hard/moder-ate/easy. Participants follow circuit round,

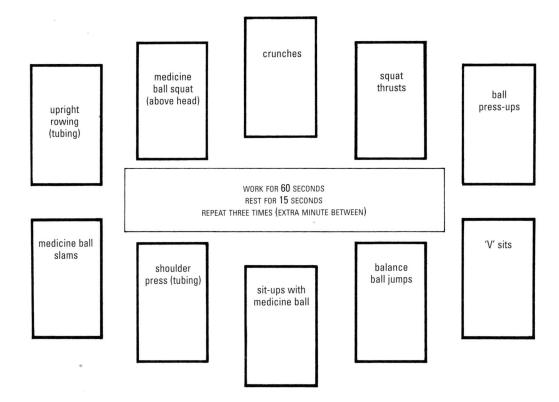

*Fig. 45. An advanced circuit.*

selecting their own intensity of work. This is highly suitable if the squad is of a varied fitness level.

*Split Circuit (T2T→ T2W)*
Swimmer moves along the line of apparatus performing predetermined repetitions on each selected apparatus in personal preferential order; no rest allowed. For example, fifteen repetitions on each exercise, then move on to the next exercise. Second time around, repetitions may change.

*Triangles/Squares (T2C→ T2W)*
Two or three triangles and/or squares of exercises within one circuit. Triangles or squares can be made up of exercises for one muscle group or as for the normal order in circuit training, e.g. three or four different abdominal exercises, then three or four shoulder exercises. This is a tough option!

*Target Circuit (T2C→ T2W)*
Swimmer chalks or writes up the maximum repetitions completed beside each exercise, thus setting the target for the next swimmer at that station. Minimum and maximum repetitions are recorded for each exercise by the coach and used the next time that circuit is performed. Good for motivating teams/squads. Make sure that all exercises are performed correctly and safely.

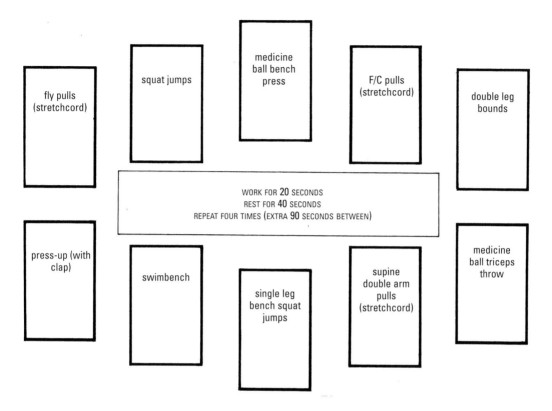

*Fig. 46. A power circuit.*

*Repeat Circuit (T2C→ T2W)*

This is when some type of exercise is completed between each exercise. A simple example is to perform ten press-ups between each exercise. This method will exercise your given target area well; however, make sure you do not place the exercise used within the circuit. It is also wise to change the exercise as soon as swimmers are finding it too difficult to perform correctly. This is also great for motivating the group and for maintaining focus on the session.

*Overtaking*

Swimmers start off at intervals and try to overtake the person in front – techniques must be correct and you should always have a minimum of two sets of equipment laid out. An excellent addition to this is to get the group to run completely around the circuit stations, then on to the next exercise. Make sure that if you use this method, your group are fit and there is sufficient space to run around.

*Team Circuit (T2C→ T2W)*

One team performs, the others rest – either time or repetitions tried to be bettered; or set teams in lines all working together. Move on to the next exercises when the whole team has finished. Good for motivating and bonding teams.

71

*Weights Circuit (T2C━▶ T2W)*

It is also possible to use circuit training within a weights gym, provided the swimmers are sufficiently experienced, there is enough space and, perhaps most importantly, exclusive use. This would only be an option if these conditions are met and with advanced swimmers, although there are better options available.

## CORE STABILITY – SWISS BALLS

Although relatively new to the fitness industry, Swiss Balls have been used in physical rehabilitation for nearly forty years. Swiss-ball training is an excellent way to build 'core-body strength' and have some fun at the same time. Training with the ball forces you to use muscles that stabilize and control the body's position. Exercises progress from simple to complex by placing the body in a more 'unstable' balance position. This forces the musculature to activate and stabilize the joints and body. This type of training provides a high level of nervous-system activation and therefore can be strenuous without ever significantly elevating the heart rate. It also encourages a transfer of power and strength through the 'kinetic chain' (i.e. the linked system of joint actions) and is a vital element of dryland training for swimming.

Swiss-ball exercises are used to develop:

- Core strength in the muscles of the trunk;
- Good postural alignment;
- Smooth and controlled movement through the kinetic chain by activating muscles fixed to the trunk;
- Joint stability and control (i.e. this reduces the likelihood of joint injury);
- Flexibility and range of motion.

Generally, Swiss-ball exercises are done slowly and with great muscular control. Most of

| Sizing Guidelines for Exercise | |
|---|---|
| **Your Height** | **Ball Size** |
| Under 5ft 2in (1.57m) | 45cm |
| 5ft 3in–5ft 8in (1.60m–1.72m) | 55cm |
| 5ft 9in–6ft 2in (1.75m–1.88m) | 65cm |
| Above 6ft 3in (1.90m) | 75cm |

the exercises also require a 'hold' position at the limits in the range of motion. Once individual exercises are learnt, they can be done in 'sets' (i.e. multiple repetitions) and then sets can be combined into a training routine.

When buying a Swiss ball, there are a few important considerations:

- It is vital that a Swiss ball will not burst if punctured, but rather slowly deflate so the user can get off the ball safely.
- Make sure the ball can take your weight and that of any external loads (e.g. dumbbells, etc.) that you might be using.
- Balls that are smooth and shiny can be difficult to stay on when you are sweaty. Choose a ball that has a textured finish, or one with a slightly 'sticky' finish.
- It is also important to choose the correct size of ball and inflate it properly; it should be firmly inflated, so that when pressed with one finger, a slight dent is created, approximately 2in (5cm) across. When seated on the ball, your thigh should be parallel or slightly above parallel to the ground.

The table above lists some optimum ball sizes based on average heights.

With careful attention, a Swiss ball can last many years. A Swiss ball is like any other piece of exercise equipment, it can be used correctly to achieve positive results or it can be used incorrectly and thus may cause injury. The following series of exercises and coaching points are intended to be used as part of a comprehensive and systematic training programme to help you swim faster.

## Getting Started – Spine Stability

Three natural curves are present in a healthy spine (Fig. 47). The neck, or the cervical spine, curves slightly inward. The mid-back, or the thoracic spine, is curved outward. The lower back, or the lumbar spine, curves inward again. The neutral alignment is important in helping to cushion the spine from too much stress and strain. Learning how to maintain a neutral spine position also helps you to move safely during activities like sitting, walking and lifting. These natural curves of the spine are created by the muscles, ligaments and tendons that attach to the vertebrae of the spine. Without these supporting structures, the spine would collapse. They support the spine – much like guide wires support the mast of a ship. This guide-wire system is made up mainly of the abdominal and back muscles. The abdominal muscles provide support by attaching to the ribs, pelvis and, indirectly, to the lumbar spine. The muscles of the back are arranged in layers, with each layer playing an important role in balancing the spine. By using these muscles together, it is possible to change the curves of the spine.

Controlling pelvic tilt is one way to begin helping to balance the spine. As certain muscles of the back and abdomen contract, the pelvis rotates. As the pelvis rotates forward, the lumbar curve increases. As the pelvis rotates backward, the curve of the lower back straightens. Rotation of the pelvis is like a wheel centred at the hip joint. The muscles of the upper thighs also attach to the pelvis and contraction of these muscles can be used to change the curve of the spine. The abdominal muscles work alone or with the hamstring

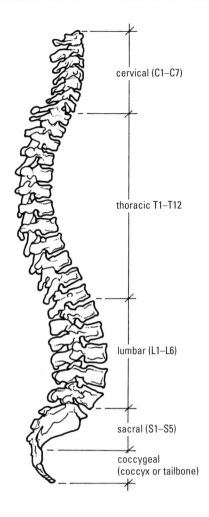

cervical (C1–C7)

thoracic T1–T12

lumbar (L1–L6)

sacral (S1–S5)

coccygeal (coccyx or tailbone)

*Fig. 47. The spinal vertebrae.*

muscles to produce a backward rotation of the pelvis. This causes the slight inward curve of the lower back to straighten. If these muscles cause the curve of the lower back to straighten too much, this may produce an unhealthy slouching posture.

In the other direction, as the hip flexors contract and back extensors contract, the pelvis is rotated forward, increasing the curvature of the lower back. If this curve is

*Fig. 48. Sitting knee lifts with extended legs.*

increased too much, another unhealthy posture may result. This condition is called lordosis in medical terminology or swayback in common terms.

A balance of strength and flexibility is the key to maintaining the neutral spine position. This balance is the basis for optimal muscle function. Like a car, an imbalance may lead to wear and tear, eventually damaging the various parts of the car. Muscle imbalances that affect the spine have many causes. One common cause of muscle imbalance is weak abdominal muscles. As the abdominal muscles sag, the hip flexors become tight, causing an increase in the curve of the low back. This leads to the swayback posture mentioned above. Another common problem results from tight hamstrings. As the hamstring muscles become tight, the pelvis is rotated backwards. This produces an abnormal slouching posture, sadly all too common in young swimmers today.

By working on spine stability (posture) you can greatly improve your chances of swimming faster by having a much more stable base to begin with, i.e. the mast and guide wires on your ship enable you to sail (swim) much more effectively and efficiently. These exercise descriptions and illustrations are designed to improve your stability and, ultimately, your swimming performance.

**Swiss-Ball Exercises**

*Balance and Stability*

*Sitting Knee Lifts with Extended Legs (Fig. 48) (SwSk)*
Sit on the top of the ball with an upright torso and feet placed flat on the ground. Slowly lift and extend one leg into the air while maintaining your body position. Repeat with the opposite leg.

*Fig. 49. Two-point balance on knees.*

### Four-Point Balance (T2T)

Kneel on top of the ball, bending over forward and placing both hands on the ground. Slowly remove one hand from the ground and maintain balance on the ball. Repeat with the opposite hand.

### Two-Point Balance on Knees (Fig. 49) (T2T)

Kneel on top of the ball, bending over forward and placing both hands on the front of the ball. Slowly remove both hands from the ball and extend the hips and knees until standing up on your knees.

### Sitting Balance (Fig. 50) (SwSk)

Sit on top of the ball with both feet flat on the ground. Slowly lift both feet off the ground and balance in this position.

### Standing Balance (Fig. 51) (T2C)

With support from a partner or the wall, establish a balanced position standing on the ball.

### Supine Knee Lift (T2T)

Lie in a supine position, placing the ball under the mid/upper back. Hips should be straight and knees bent at 90 degrees. Slowly lift one leg into the air.

### One-Ball Press-Up (Fig. 52) (T2C)

Begin in the press-up bridge with both hands on the ball. Feet should be together, but a more stable starting position may be with the feet apart.

### Two-Ball Press-Up (T2C)

Begin in the press-up position, placing a ball under each hand and with feet in a stable position. Perform a press-up.

*Fig. 50. Sitting balance.*

*Fig. 51. Standing balance.*

### Legs and Hips

*Back Wall Squats (SwSk)*
Place the ball against the wall behind you and centred at your waist; step forward 12–14in, keeping your feet at about a shoulder-width stance. Keeping the back straight, squat down rolling the ball behind you until the knees reach a 90-degree angle. Extend the legs to return to the upright starting position.

Advanced variations:
- Use one leg (T2C);
- One leg with the free leg extended (T2C);
- Hold dumb-bells at your sides or at shoulder level. (T2W).

*Front Wall Squats (SwSk)*
Place the ball against the wall in front you at waist height. Step backward to allow for a comfortable forward lean (approximately 65–70 degrees). Standing on your tip-toes with a shoulder-width stance, squat down allowing your hips to move backward. During the movement, stand on the balls of your

*Fig. 52. One ball press-up.*

feet, keeping your ankles bent at 90 degrees. Arms should hang down to your sides, or grab the ball for extra stability.

Variations:
- Use one leg (T2C);
- Hold dumb-bells at your sides or at shoulder level (T2W).

### One Leg Squat with Mobility (T2C)
Stand upright with one leg on the ground and the opposite leg supported by the ball. The hip of the supported leg should be flexed slightly, with the toes on the ball. Slowly bend down with the ground-based leg, while extending the supported leg (this will require a forward lean of the torso), the ball should roll from the toes to the shin of the supported leg. Return to the starting position by standing up with the ground-based leg, returning contact to the toes of the supported leg.

### Prone Two-Leg Extension (Fig. 53) (T2T)
Begin by resting your forearms on the ground in a prone position, while placing your feet on the ball. Keep your entire body straight. Slowly flex your hips and knees until the

Fig. 53. Prone two-leg extension.

knees almost touch the ground. Return to the starting position by straightening your legs completely, paying strict attention to keeping your body completely straight.
  Variations:
• Prone one-leg extension (T2C);
• Prone one-leg extension on your toes (T2C).

*Supine Two-Leg Curls (Fig. 54) (T2T)*
Lie in a prone position by supporting your upper body on your shoulders and with arms held out to the sides. Place your heels on the top of the ball, keeping your legs completely straight. Slowly bend your legs while keeping your torso in the starting position. Return to the starting position by extending your legs.
  Variations:
• Supine one-leg curl (T2C);
• Supine one-leg curl with mobility (alternate flexion and extension with each leg) (T2C).

**Abdominals and Obliques**

*Floor Crunches – Feet on Ball (T2T)*
Lie on your back with your feet placed on the ball (hips and knees should be at a 90-degree angle). Hands can be placed across the chest. Slowly contract your abdominals to raise the shoulders off the ground. Relax your abdominals to return to the starting position.
  Variations:
• Place hands behind the head (T2T);
• Place arms straight out past the head (T2C).

*Supine Rotations (T2C)*
Lie on your back with your feet placed on the ball (hips and knees should form a 90-degree angle); arms should be out to the sides to aid in support. Slowly rotate the hips to either side while maintaining the leg position (rotate as far as the individual's ROM will allow). Complete the movement by rotating the hips completely to the other side.
  Variation:
• Lift the ball off the ground during the entire ROM.

*Floor Reverse Crunches (T2T)*
Lie on your back with your feet placed on the ball (hips and knees should form a 90-degree angle); arms should be held out to the sides to aid in support. Slowly lift the ball off the ground as far as your ROM will allow. Return the ball to the starting position.
  Variation:
• Twist and crunch: perform the movement the same way except, during the hip flexion, perform a twisting motion (T2C).

*Fig. 54 Supine two-leg curls.*

*Floor Full Crunches (T2T)*
Lie on your back with your feet placed on the ball (hips and knees should form a 90-degree angle), place hands across the chest. Slowly lift the ball off the ground and touch your elbows to your knees. Return the ball and shoulders to the ground.
    Variations:
- Place hands behind your head (T2C);
- Hold arms straight past the head (T2C).

*Partial Abdominal Crunch (Fig. 55) (T2T)*
Lie flat on the ball (ball should be centred with the lower back) with your feet placed flat on the ground. Place hands across the chest. Bring the torso up to a 45-degree angle by contracting the abdominals and hip flexors. Lower back to the starting position.
    Variations:
- Place hands behind the head (T2C);
- Hold arms straight out past the head (T2C);
- Add a twisting motion during the upward phase (T2C).

*Full Abdominal Crunch (T2T)*
Lie flat on the ball (ball should be centred with the lower back) with your feet placed flat on the ground. Place hands across the chest. Bring the torso up to a 90-degree angle by contracting the abdominals and hip flexors. Lower back to the starting position.

Fig. 55. Partial abdominal crunch.

*Fig. 56. Three-point prone hyperextensions.*

Variations:
- Place hands behind the head (T2C);
- Hold arms straight out past the head (T2C);
- Add a twisting motion during the upward phase (T2C).

### Two-Leg Bridges (SwSk)
Lie flat on your back, resting your arms across your chest and place your heels on the stability ball. Lift your hips off the ground until your body is aligned.

### Hip Lifts Supported on Balls of Feet (T2T)
Lie on your back with your arms held out to the sides. Place the balls of your feet flat on the side of the stability ball, keeping the knees slightly bent. Lift your hips off the ground until your body is aligned.
Variation:
- Use one foot: keep the free leg extended in the air (T2C).

### Triple-Threat Combination (T2C)
Lie flat on your back, resting your arms across your chest and place your heels on the stabil-ity ball. Perform a two-leg bridge, supine leg curl and hip lift on the balls of your feet; three repetitions, each in succession.
Variation:
- Same as above using one leg (T2C).

### Kneeling Prone Hyperextensions (T2T)
Kneel down and place the stability ball under your body with your hands behind your head. Lift your torso off the ball to an angle of about 45 degrees.
Variation:
- Hold the arms extended out past the head (T2C).

### Three-Point Prone Hyperextensions (Fig. 56) (T2C)
Lie face down on the stability ball, with legs extended, and balance on the toes of your feet. The ball should be placed under the stomach and the hands held behind the head. Lift the torso in the air, keeping the toes on the ground.
Variation:
- Hold the arms extended out past the head (T2C).

Fig. 57. Supine ball lift.

## Reverse Hyperextensions (T2C)

Lie face down over the stability ball with your arms folded under your head. The lower body should be balanced on the toes. Lift the legs into the air by extending the hips. The weight of the body should be balanced on the ground using the arms.

## One-Leg Reverse Hyperextension (T2C)

Balance the weight of the upper body on the hands on the floor. Flex the hips to a 90-degree angle, while balancing the knee and shin of one leg on the ball, with the other leg held straight resting on the ball. Lift the free leg all the way up into the air, keeping it straight.

Variation:
- Use one leg while balancing on the toes (T2C).

### Hip Flexion – Abdominals/Obliques

## Supine Ball Lift (Fig. 57) (T2T)

Lie on your back while placing the stability ball between the feet. Arms should be held at the sides. Lift the ball off the ground to an angle of about 90 degrees, keeping the knees straight. Alternately lift and lower straight up and down, or lift and lower to each side.

## Lateral Lying Ball Lift (T2T)

Lie on your side placing the ball between the feet. Lift the ball off the ground to an angle of about 45 degrees.

## Flexed-Knee Ball Exchange (T2T)

Lie on your back while placing the stability ball between the feet. Hands should be placed straight out past the head. Lift the ball up to the body by bending the knees. At the same time, use the arms to reach and exchange the ball from the feet to the hands. Once exchanged, return the arms and legs to the starting position. Complete the movement by returning the ball to the feet.

Variation:
- Use straight legs during the exchange (T2C).

## Prone Leg Tucks – Two Legs (Fig. 58) (T2T)

Start in the push-up position with the knees balanced on top of the ball, elbows extended and the weight of the body supported by the arms. Curl the knees up towards the body.

Variations:
- Use one leg: free leg should be extended straight out over the ball;
- Balance your toes on the ball (T2C).

## Prone Leg Rolls (T2C)

Start in the push-up position with the knees balanced on top of the ball, elbows extended and the weight of the body supported by the arms. Roll onto the side of each leg while maintaining the upper body position. (Keep legs together throughout the exercise.)

## Prone J Strokes (T2C)

Start in the push-up position with the knees balanced on top of the ball, elbows extended and the weight of the body supported by the arms. Roll onto the side of each leg, while tucking the knees into the body.

## Prone Skiers on Two Legs (T2C)

Knees and hips should be flexed to a 90-degree angle with the knees resting on the ball. Hands should be on the ground with the elbows fully extended. Twist the lower body from side to side rolling onto the sides of the knees. Maintain the upper body position.

Variation:
- Use one leg: same as above, except the free leg is held out over the ball and the knee of the free leg is slightly bent.

## Hip Twisters (T2C)

Start in the push-up position, placing the ball under the knees and upper thighs. Roll the hips

*Fig. 58. Prone leg tucks – two legs.*

to one side (*see* Fig. 2, page 9). Once positioned on your side, hyperextend the top leg.

*Prone Upper Body Rocking (T2T)*
Lie face down on the stability ball, hips and knees straight and balanced on the toes. Hug the ball. Rock from side to side, touching the ground with the forearm on each side.

*Prone Pike – Two Legs (Fig. 59) (T2T)*
Start in the push-up position, with your knees resting on top of the stability ball. Raise your hips up to form a 90-degree angle, while rolling onto your toes.
  Variation:
• Use one leg (T2C).

*Hip Roll-Outs on Knees (Fig. 60) (T2T)*
Kneel down and sit back. Arms should be straight and hands placed on the ball. Roll forward over the ball by extending the hips and knees. Body should almost be aligned.
  Variation:
• Hip roll out on your toes: straight line from the hands to the hips.

*Shoulder Roll-Outs (T2C)*
Kneel down on the ground with the hips straight, arms extended and hands on the ball. The torso should have a forward lean of about 45 degrees. Then roll forward over the ball onto the forearms by extending the knees. Continue to keep the hips straight

*Fig. 59. Prone pike – two legs.*

throughout the exercise. The body should almost be aligned at the bottom of the movement.

*Hip Roll-Outs on Your Feet (T2T)*
Stand with your feet flat on the ground, hips flexed to a 90-degree angle and your arms extended straight over your head with hands placed on the ball. Slowly allow the hips to completely straighten out. The body should be aligned at the bottom of the movement. Return to the starting position by flexing the hips, keeping the knees straight.

## Chest

*Protraction/Retraction with Two Legs (T2C)*
Start in the press-up position with shins and feet resting on the ball. Keeping the body aligned and elbows locked, slowly allow the scapulae to pull in, pause, then extend.
Variation:
• Use one leg.

*Walk-Outs with Two Legs (T2T)*
Kneel down on both knees with the ball placed under the body and hands placed on

*Fig. 60. Hip roll-outs on knees.*

the ground. Begin by 'walking' forward on your hands using small steps. As you move forward, the ball will travel/roll under the hips and legs. Keep the body tight and aligned.

Variations:
- Use one leg (T2C);
- Clock walks with two legs: as per walk-outs except when ball is near feet, using your hands, walk in a 180–360-degree circle (T2C).

*Press-Up Progression with Two Legs on Ball (T2C) (Fig. 61)*
Begin in the press-up position with the ball placed under the hips and hands placed on

the ground. Keeping the body completely aligned perform a press-up.

Progression:
- Ball under:
  hips;
  thighs;
  knees:
  feet;
  toes.
- As above but with one leg.

*Press-Up with Hands on Ball, Feet on Floor (T2C)*
Begin in the push-up position, with the body completely aligned, hands placed on the ball and body balanced on the toes. Perform a

*Fig. 61. Press-up progression with two legs on ball.*

push-up keeping perfect body alignment and avoiding scapular retraction.

Variations:
- Hands on ball, feet elevated;
- One hand on ball, feet on the ground;
- Place a ball under each hand, feet on the ground.

### Shoulders

*Knee Tuck Press (T2C)*
Begin in the press-up position, with the ball placed under the knees and hands on the ground. Tuck the knees up to the body; the ball should roll and stop under the shins. Once the knees are in a tuck position, move hands forward about 15–20cm (6–8in). Perform a shoulder press.

Variation:
- Use a larger ball.

*Pike Press (T2C)*
Begin in the press-up position with the ball placed under the knees/shins, and hands placed on the ground. Keeping the knees extended, flex the hips to a 90-degree angle. Perform a shoulder press.

Variations:
- Use a larger ball;
- Use one leg.

### External Resistance

*Dumb-Bell Flat Press (Fig. 62) (T2C)*
Lie in a prone position, placing the ball centred under the upper back. Knees should be

*Fig. 62. Dumb-bell flat press.*

bent to a 90-degree angle, and dumb-bells held at the sides of the chest. Press the dumb-bells up to full elbow extension; maintain body position on the ball.

*Dumb-Bell Flat Fly (Fig. 63) (T2C)*
Lie in a prone position, placing the ball centred under the low back. Knees should be bent to a 90-degree angle, and dumb-bells held over the chest with elbows slightly flexed. Slowly allow the dumb-bells to lower to each side, while keeping the elbows slightly bent. Lower until the dumb-bells reach chest level, and then bring back to the starting position.

*Fig. 63. Dumb-bell flat fly.*

*Dumb-Bell Sitting Overhead Press (T2C)*
Sit on top of the ball with the knees and hips bent at 90-degree angles, and dumb-bells held at shoulder level. While seated on the ball, perform a shoulder press by completely extending the elbows.

Variations:
• Alternate arm presses;
• Alternate arm presses with mobility (rock side to side);
• Use one arm.

*Dumb-Bell Sitting Lateral Raise with Two Arms (T2C)*
Sit on top of the ball with the knees and hips bent at 90-degree angles and dumb-bells held

at the sides. While seated on the ball, perform a lateral raise by abducting both arms. Raise the dumb-bells just above shoulder level.

Variations:
- Alternate arms;
- Alternate arms with mobility (rock side to side);
- Use one arm.

### Dumb-Bell Sitting Front Raise with One Arm (T2C)

Sit on top of the ball with the knees and hips bent at 90-degree angles and dumb-bells held at the sides. While seated on the ball, perform a front raise by flexing the shoulders. Raise each dumb-bell just above shoulder level.

Variation:
- Raise both arms simultaneously.

### Dumb-Bell Sitting Front/Lateral Raise (T2C)

Sit on top of the ball with the knees and hips bent at 90-degree angles, and dumb-bells held at the sides. Simultaneously perform a front raise with one arm, and a lateral raise with the other arm.

### Dumb-Bell Sitting Upright Rows Two Arms Alternating (T2C)

Sit on top of the ball using a wide foot stance and holding the dumb-bells out in front and in between the legs. Lean slightly forward. While seated, perform an upright row with the right arm, bringing the dumb-bell up to the armpit. While lowering the dumb-bell, simultaneously raise the other dumb-bell held in the left hand.

### Rotator Cuff Circuit (T2T)

Sit on top of the ball holding the rubber cord in either hand. While maintaining an upright torso, perform internal/external rotations, as shown in Fig. 43, page 67.

### Seated Row (T2C)

Sit on top of the ball using a wide foot stance and knees bent to 90 degrees. Wrap a rubber-resistance cord around a stable object; grasp the handles with the arms extended and an upright torso. Keeping the torso upright, pull both arms simultaneously toward the body.

### Dumb-Bell Row – Chest on Ball (T2C)

Lie in a prone position placing the ball under the chest. Legs should be extended, and arms held out at a 90-degree angle holding the dumb-bells. Lift the elbows high into the air while maintaining a 90-degree shoulder angle.

### Dumb-Bell Pullover (Fig. 64) (T2C)

Lie in a supine position with the ball placed under the upper back, hips straight and knees bent to 90 degrees. Hold the dumb-bells just over the chest. Slowly allow the dumb-bells to lower behind the head. Keep the elbows in and slightly bent. Return to the starting position.

## MEDICINE BALLS

You have probably seen those old-time photos of muscle men in briefs holding a weighted, leather ball called a medicine ball. For centuries, muscle men used the heavy spheres to increase muscle mass and improve co-ordination, but after years of being side-lined by step-platforms and spinning bikes, medicine balls have been rediscovered by the contemporary fitness enthusiast, and swimming coaches are no exception. Originally these strength-building globes were stuffed with rags, had no bounce and were very loose and floppy, making them a little hard to handle. But today's manufacturers have utilized modern materials such as gel to fill the brawny balls, making them much more versatile and easy to catch.

*Fig. 64. Dumb-bell pullover.*

Today's medicine balls are available in a variety of shapes, sizes, materials, colours and weights, and their new versatility enhances the effectiveness of any training programme. Incorporating medicine-ball work into your regular exercise routine is a must for all swimmers. Just like Swiss-ball work, medicine-ball training is categorized as functional training, which means it integrates multiple muscles or muscle groups to complete a movement and mimics everyday muscle use. Because the body is a complicated and integrated system of muscles, nerves, pathways, bones, joints and other connective tissues that work together to create movement, training it as such can be much more beneficial than isolating muscle groups. An added plus is that you must engage the core muscles to stabilize the torso and prevent back injuries, making this training a perfect workout for the back, abdomen and hips.

When most people think of a medicine ball, they usually get a mental picture of the old, tattered and torn brown leather weighted ball sitting in the corner of an old-school iron-pumping gym. They also see these balls as being a very outdated method of working out. When was the last time you saw anyone use one of those or even heard anyone talk about them? With all the modern exercise machines and other various equipment available today, what possible reason could anyone have for including the medicine ball in their workout?

First of all, the medicine ball has come a long way from the old leather ones mentioned earlier. They now come in a vast array of colours and are made with rubber surfaces making them easier to grip. They also come in weights ranging from one to fifty pounds, so you can vary resistance to suit your needs. Because they bounce and can be tossed around, they are great for working you with random movements instead of the fixed ones that come with bar-bell, dumb-bell and machine workouts. There is virtually no other equipment in the gym or at home that can provide the versatility of the medicine ball.

You can add variety to your routine because of the limitless kinds of exercises you can do with them. You can toss them, bounce them, roll them and do many traditional free-weight exercises with them. With all the variety they provide, it is hard to get bored with their use and everyone can benefit from using them.

A lot of medicine-ball exercises are great for working your core or mid-section mus-cles, which are involved when you toss, roll, bounce or catch it. There is also a lot of movement involved when using the ball, like side to side movement or front to back movement, to catch it. Standing and twisting side to side while holding the ball is great for your mid-section as well. Probably the most famous and successful exponent of medicine ball in swimming was Olympic champion, world champion and former world-record holder on breaststroke, Mike Barrowman. Regularly programming medicine-ball work into his weekly routine, Barrowman continues to promote this form of 'plyometric' training through books and videos. The word plyometric is apparently derived from the Greek and means to increase, or do more and measure. It was extensively used by Soviet and Eastern Bloc athletes in the 1960s and 1970s and first appeared 'in the West' in 1975 via esteemed US athletics coach, Fred Wilt. It is interesting to note that Mike Barrowman's coach Josef Nagy is Hungarian.

Some people have questioned the use of 'plyometric' training for swimmers, putting forward the notion that it might only be useful for improving starts and turns. But this would be to misrepresent what plyometrics is and can be to the competitive swimmer. A narrow view of plyometrics would be to see it just as jumps and bounds, but applying the same principles to the upper body can be just as beneficial. The most useful analogy is to see plyometrics as a 'bridge' between any strength gains made on land and performance improvements in the water. It seems clear from what little research there is that getting stronger on land does not have a direct correlation to swimming faster, so building such a 'bridge' is both conceptually sound and makes good 'training' sense. Mixed or 'complex' training is a staple of swimming coaches in the pool, with the blend of swim, kick, pull, drills, intensities of work, each of the

Fig. 65 Russian twist.

strokes and so on. The application of this principle on land allows the effective coach to combine plyometric training with other methods to best effect.

## Medicine-Ball Exercises

*Russian Twist (Fig. 65) (T2T)*
Begin by holding the ball at belly-button height, arm's length away from the body and behind your right or left hip. Start by moving ball to the right or left. Keep the core tight and turn/rotate back foot to allow greater range of motion on exercise.

*Diagonal Chops (Fig. 66) (T2T)*
Start with ball behind and above ear, then move the ball diagonally across the body, ending near knee of opposite leg or foot. Return with same pattern. Rotate/turn back foot to increase effective range of exercise.

*Figure of Eight #1 (Fig. 67) (SwSk)*
Begin with ball at ear level and arms extended. Move the ball through a figure of eight pattern continuously. Pattern will be in front and side of body taking you from right to left.

*Chops (SwSk)*
Start with ball overhead at arm's length. Stop the ball when it is between your feet. Repeat.

*Circles (SwSk)*
Begin with ball overhead and move ball in a circular motion, as big as possible around your body.

Fig. 66. Diagonal chops.

Fig. 67. Figure of eight #1.

Fig. 68. Medicine-ball squat.

*Single Leg Russian Twist (T2T)*
*See* Russian twist exercise. When weight is off
the back leg, take it off the ground.

*Single Leg Chop (T2T)*
*See* diagonal-chop exercise. Balance on one
leg and perform the exercise.

*Medicine-Ball Squat (Figs 68 and 69) (SwSk)*
Keep ball at arm's length while performing a
squat. A possible variation is to start with the
ball at your chest and press up or out when
squatting, returning to chest on ascent (*see*
Fig. 69).

*Medicine-Ball Lunge #1 and #2 (Figs 70
and 71) (T2T)*
Begin with ball at belly-button level. Take a
step forward with one leg. At the same time,
move the ball to side of lunging leg. Continue alternating legs by either walking or
switching in place (*see* Fig. 71).

Fig. 69. Squat with ball above head.

95

*Fig. 70. Medicine-ball lunge #1.*

*Medicine-Ball Lunge #3 (Fig. 72) (T2T)*
Begin with ball at belly button. While lunging forward, raise the ball up overhead. Either leave the ball overhead while continuing to lunge or return ball to belly button on each lunge.

*Sagittal or Front Reach (SwSk)*
Begin with ball at belly button. Step forward and extend arms to touch or approach front foot. Return and repeat in place with same foot, or alternate.

*Frontal or Side Reach (SwSk)*
Begin with ball at belly button. Step and laterally reach to one side. Continue reaching and stepping to one side, or alternate legs.

*Transverse or Rear Reach (SwSk)*
Start with ball at belly button. Open and step/reach between 90 and 180 degrees to the rear. Return to start and repeat with same leg or opposite leg.

*One-Leg Squat (T2T)*
Start with ball at arm's length. Squat on one leg with ball held out in front as a counterbalance. Leave free leg in front. Can also be done by leaving free leg to side or rear. Ball can start from belly button and be pressed out when squatting.

*Medicine-Ball Press-Up (T2C)*
Position ball under one hand and perform a press-up. Try doing one press-up with hand

*Fig. 71. Medicine-ball lunge #2.*

*Fig. 72. Medicine-ball lunge #3.*

*Fig. 73. Figure of eight #2.*

*Fig. 74. Triceps press.*

on ground, pushing hard enough to catch yourself on the ball for next repetition. Begin to roll ball across to opposite hand between repetitions if you want a bigger challenge.

*Figure of Eight #2 (Fig. 73) (SwSk)*
Stand with your feet greater than shoulder-width apart. Pass the ball around your ankles in a figure-of-eight pattern. Remember to go both ways.

*Triceps Press (Fig. 74) (SwSk)*
Hold the ball above your head, keeping your elbows in, perform a triceps press by lowering and raising the ball behind you head. Great as a warm-up exercise.

*Chest Pass (Fig. 75) (SwSk)*
Work in pairs. Stand facing your partner. Hold the ball in front of your chest with your elbows bent. Push the ball out with both hands in a vigorous basketball/netball passing action and throw to your partner. If both swimmers

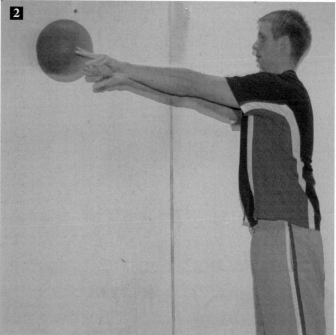

*Fig. 75. Chest pass.*

are sufficiently skilled, a continuous passing action can be performed with successive receiving and passing movements for a set time or number of repetitions. By combining with either a standing squat or a sit-up, this exercise can be further developed.

*Overhead Triceps Throw (Fig. 76) (T2T)*
Work in pairs. Pull in the abdominals at the start. Fix the spine. Throw the ball to your partner's chest in a soccer 'throw in' motion. Keep the movements smooth and slow. Stay upright, keep the knees over the toes and not in front of them. To make the exercise more challenging, perform in a kneeling position. If both swimmers are skilled, the throws can be made directly to the starting position each time and not to the chest. Add a further variation by including a squat before the throw each time.

*Fig. 76. Overhead triceps throw.*

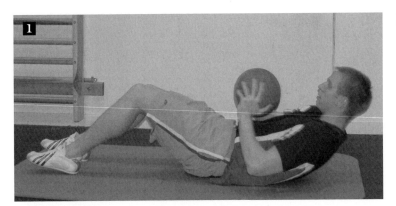

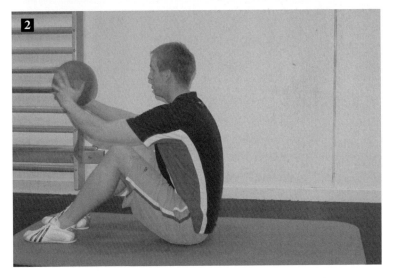

*Fig. 77. Sit-up #1.*

*Bench Press Pass (T2T)*

Work in pairs. Lie on the floor holding both hands upwards ready to receive the ball. Partner drops the ball and as the hands receive the ball, lower it to the chest and rapidly return it to the partner in a bench-press-type action. Well-skilled swimmers will be able to perform this in a rhythmical, continuous manner.

*Single-Arm Throw (T2T)*

Work in pairs. Stand side on to your partner. Throw single-handed to your partner, pushing through the ball quickly. Rotate the torso to increase power.

*Slams (T2C)*

Start with the ball overhead. Throw directly downwards by pulling the ball down with your mid-section. Keep ball stretched as long as possible. This exercise can also be done with one arm.

*Start Throws (T2T)*

Begin with weight evenly distributed between feet and hands. Deliver ball by pushing on ground with feet and bringing ball to position near chest. As you are completing hip extension, deliver the ball and in the direction of the throw begin running.

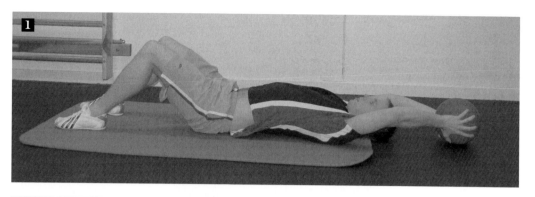

Fig. 78. Sit-up #2.

### Squat Throw #1 (T2T)

Start with ball at chest. Quickly squat and jump delivering the ball as high as possible directly overhead. Let the ball bounce once, reposition and repeat.

### Squat Throw #2 (T2T)

Start with ball at belly button or overhead. Quickly squat to have the ball at calf level. Jump and throw the ball directly overhead, letting the ball bounce once, then repeat.

### Sit-Up #1 (Fig. 77) (SwSk)

Perform a regular sit-up with bent knees, keeping the ball close to you at all times. As mentioned, this can be done with a partner

and combined with a chest pass for a more challenging exercise.

### Sit-Up #2 (Fig. 78) (T2T)

As before, but keeping the ball overhead to increase the length of the lever and make the exercise much harder.

### Lying Throw (Fig. 79) (T2T)

This can be done with a partner or for distance. Lying on your back, hold the ball out behind you with straight arms and throw powerfully with two arms. (This exercise is also shown in Fig. 1, page 8, where it is being performed by a squad of age-group swimmers.)

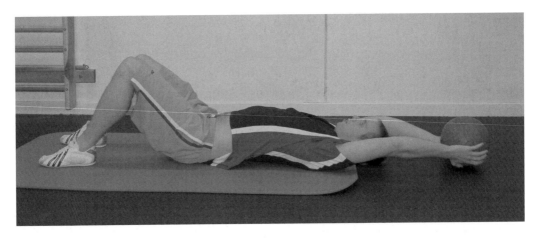

*Fig. 79. Lying throw.*

*Over the Back Throw (T2C)*
Start with ball overhead and bring it down to knees. Begin throw as soon as ball gets to knee level. Throw by extending ankle, knee, hip and delivering ball overhead backwards. You can make this a great total-body power test by measuring the distance thrown each time.

## SWIMBENCH AND STRETCHCORDS

Integral to land training at the élite level is the swimbench, which along with other on-deck devices is really about simulating the swimming actions on land. Coaches are convinced that swimbenches are one of the many ways to transfer weight-training strength gains to the pool. The two main benches of choice are the VASA Trainer and the Biokinetic Swim-Bench. At many US university programmes, swimmers will do between 45 and 75 minutes of dryland per day, including 10 to 15 minutes every other day on the bench. The benches produce two very different effects. On the Biokinetic Swim-Bench, swimmers move their arms in patterns identical to the various swim-ming strokes. It is an exercise modality that can duplicate the swimming motion with speed, with the result that acceleration capability is built into the product. This function reflects its creator's (Evan Flavell) early association with renowned scientist/coach, Doc Counsilman, who espoused exercising at speed and invented the first ever swimbench, an Isokinetic machine, i.e. exercising at a constant speed. Number-crunching coaches are particularly fond of the dynamic force and strength analysis possible with the Biokinetic bench. A simple connection allows coaches to get computer readouts that calculate and graph power output for every pull. British Swimming has a swimbench test protocol for both power and endurance as part of their sports science support programme. The power test is done over ten maximal double-arm pulls and the endurance test simulates a 200m race by lasting two minutes.

The VASA Trainer operates on a sled that rolls on a track and comes equipped with all sorts of cords, straps, pulleys and accessories. It is proponents like the variable resistance and different angles of attack and settings that make both prone and supine use possible.

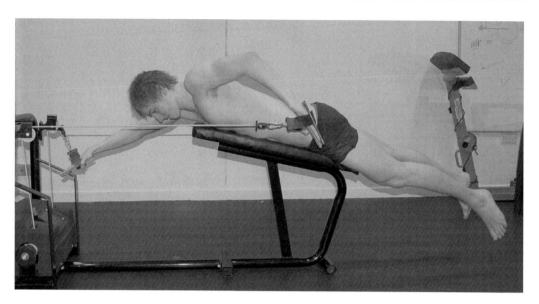

*Fig. 80. A biokinetic swimbench.*

Some coaches purchase the VASA machine for the training effect, but then find a bonus in the area of technique instruction. Not only does the swimmer get to anchor their hands and move their body past the hands, as they would in the water, but it is also possible to correct the common fault in all freestyle swimmers across the world – dropped elbows. The VASA Trainer applications also allow breaststrokers and flyers to set a high elbow and can (with some manipulation and practice) allow breaststrokers to work on deep kicks. The VASA Trainer also has a pulley-cable system that allows the user to swim in place doing freestyle. The pulley system allows for complete range of motion of the arms in freestyle and enables coach and swimmer to analyse arm strokes and correct flaws.

---

**Top Tip**

Use the bench with a mirror to check your technique.

---

It can be agreat teacher for backstroke because it gives the swimmer a good feel for the upsweep and finish. And for all strokes, it teaches the swimmer to finish all the way through, giving a direct correlation for distance per stroke in the water.

Swimbenches are not cheap and, therefore, not for everyone. The Biokinetic Swim-Bench retails for around US $3,000. The VASA Trainers are about a third of this price. Unquestionably, they are expensive devices and permit use by only one swimmer at a time. So with economic realities in mind, some coaches prefer more basic methods with the use of surgical tubing and cords. The use of swimbenches at LTAD stages will largely be determined by physical size in the first instance. Some swimmers will simply be too small to 'fit on' the bench and would be better suited to work with tubing/cords.

Essentially a giant rubber band, stretch-cords are tubes made of rubber with varying degrees of thickness according to ability and

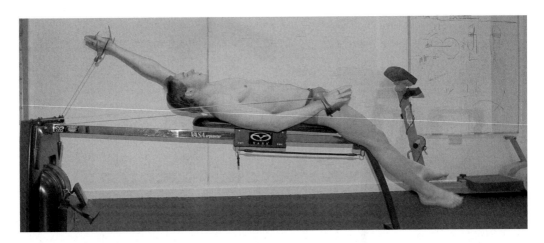

*Fig. 81. A VASA trainer.*

*Fig. 82. A stretchcord with added device.*

training requirements. The idea behind stretchcord training is to pull on the band as you would pull through the water in your strokes, with the resistance providing a workout that closely simulates the resistance you feel in the water.

There are commercially available stretchcords that are colour-coded according to thickness. Some have fabric loops on each end for your hands; some have hand-paddles already attached and others have circular devices to allow for greater flexibility of application (*see* Fig. 82). A more basic (and considerably cheaper) approach would be to use surgical tubing and attach an old set of hand-paddles. To start with, find a stable base to loop your cord around, slightly higher than waist height. At a pinch, a doorknob will do, but it is preferable to find something more stable, such as the backstroke flags or a set of wall bars in the gym. Attach it slightly higher than waist height and you are ready to go.

Begin your stretchcord work by standing away from your base with your arms extended in front of you so that the cord you are holding is taut but not tense. Start pulling the stretchcord simultaneously back past

*Fig. 83. Butterfly pull with a stretchcord.*

your hips, as if you are doing an underwater butterfly pull. When your arms are extended behind you, i.e. at the end of your stroke, bring them back in front of you in a controlled, but fast, motion (essentially backtrack your hands under your body the way they came). This is the simplest exercise of all (*see* Fig. 83). You can repeat this motion for a set time or number of strokes. A good way of regulating this type of exercise is to simulate the time and/or strokes you would take for a particular race distance, e.g. 100m fly in 70 seconds with fifty strokes.

If you have never done stretchcord training before, you may find your lower back will ache from the strain of bending over at the waist for long periods at a time. Your shoulders will also feel sore, more so than after a swim session. This is to be expected; you are exercising the muscles in a slightly different way and will soon get used to the change. A not-so-good thing is if your inner shoulder (rotator cuff area) begins to ache. This is an indicator that you are straining your shoulders too much and/or not doing the drill correctly. If you are jerking the cord back and allowing the tension to pull your arms back above your head rather than bringing your arms back in a controlled motion, you are doing more harm than good.

Another thing to watch out for is tubing that can snap or break. Because bands are rubber, make sure your base is not abrasive (such as a rough tree or a fencepost with a sharp surface). Always check your tubing at the midway

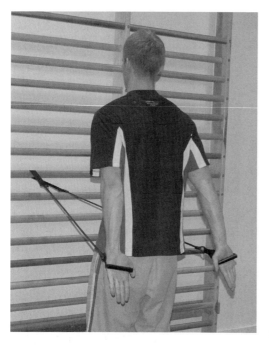

*Fig. 84. Triceps pushback.*

and base point for cracks and rips that could result in a snapped fragment. When you tie it around your base, you may want to loop it around at the halfway point double, and bring the ends through the loop in the middle (this will prevent additional chafing).

Hand blisters are another side-effect of band training. Run-of-the-mill cycling or weight training gloves are ideal to prevent blistering, but best of all are swimming paddles attached to the band handle grips; this not only prevents chafing but allows for a more accurate simulation of the underwater phase of the stroke.

Tubing does not have to be limited to the butterfly/freestyle (*see* Fig. 5, page 11) underwater motion either. You can attempt the same drill with a breaststroke pull, or you can lie down on your back with your head pointing toward your tubing base and pull your arms down to work on your backstroke pull. You can even affix the tubing to your

*Fig. 85. Push forwards #1.*

*Fig. 86. Push forwards #2.*

feet and practise breaststroke kicking. These additional exercises are shown in Figs 84–90.

*Triceps Pushback (Fig. 84) (T2T)*
Stand with feet hip-width apart; knees bent and abdominals tight. Ensure there is tension on the tubing/cord before you begin. Keeping the arms straight, move both arms backwards as far as possible. Control the return of the tubing to the start position (this can be done one arm at a time, if preferred).

*Push Forwards (Figs 85 and 86) (T2T)*
Perform exactly the same movement as before, but stand facing the other way, i.e. away from the wall. In variation #1 the palms face forward (Fig. 85). In variation #2 (Fig. 86) the palms face backward and the back of the hand moves forward.

*Upright Row (Fig. 87) (T2C)*
Stand with feet together, knees slightly bent and abdominals tight. Securely stand on the

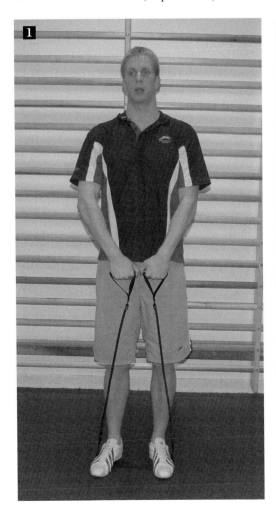

*Fig. 87. Upright row.*

 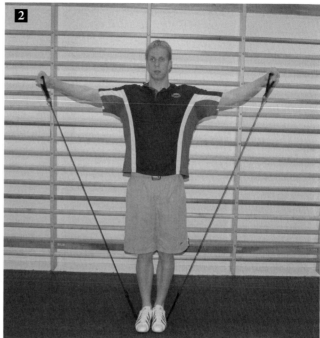

*Fig. 88. Side lateral raise.*

tubing with both feet. Keeping the elbows higher than the hands at all times, perform an upright 'rowing' pull until the hands reach the chin. Control the lowering and repeat.

*Side Lateral Raise (Fig. 88) (T2C)*
Stand with feet together; knees slightly bent and abdominals tight. Securely stand on the tubing with both feet. Keeping the arms straight, lift both arms directly to the side up to 90 degrees. Control the return.

*Front Raise (Fig. 89) (T2C)*
Stand with feet hip-width apart; knees bent and abdominals tight. Keeping the arms straight, lift both arms directly to the front. Control the return. Only lift to shoulder height.

*Lying Bent-Arm Triceps Press (Fig. 90) (T2T)*
Lie on your back and affix the tubing at a point just above the height of the body. Maintain tension and perform a triceps press with the elbows tight against the body at all times.

## RESISTANCE TRAINING

It was established in the early part of this book that it was not going to be a 'lift weights, get strong and swim fast' text. The main elements of this training section have been aimed at the majority of swimmers who do not have access to free weights or sophisticated equipment. But it would be an omission if some attention was not paid to key resistance exercises that can be of benefit to swimmers.

*Fig. 89. Front raise.*

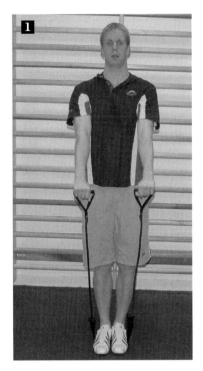

*Fig. 90. Lying bent-arm triceps press.*

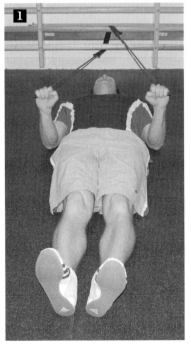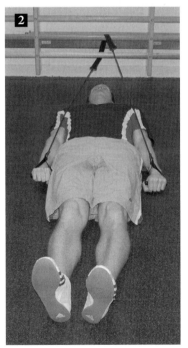

## Safe and Successful Weight Training

The human body is an extremely adaptable organism and will respond specifically to the stresses placed upon it. Unlike most man-made machines, the more you do, the more you will be capable of doing; and the less you do, the less you will be capable of doing. With this concept as a guide, the three main principles that must be applied in order to develop an effective and efficient weight-training programme are: overload, progression and regularity.

Proper lifting technique is a must if you are to receive the maximum results from your efforts. Always start out with sufficient warm-up sets and technique sets to establish correct form. Once the movement of the lift has been mastered, you will be ready to advance and move to heavier weights. Never sacrifice form and technique to try a weight that is heavier than you are ready to handle. When approaching muscular failure, remember to maintain proper lifting technique and allow your training partner (spotter) to help you through the final repetitions. Proper breathing is an important part of lifting technique. Inhale while lowering the weight to get more balanced overall muscle development, and exhale as you complete the lift. The result is greater functional strength. The spotter is also very important to your lifting success. The spotters must pay attention so they know when and how much assistance is needed. Proper spotting technique is necessary so the lifter can maintain good lifting form and position. Two hands should be used with an alternate (opposing) grip when spotting press lifts and most other moves. Spotting the squat requires two people, one at each end of the bar. The spotter is necessary to prevent injuries to the lifter and to others in the immediate area.

The principle of progression is important not only for efficient progress, but also for maximum safety. You should always set your starting workload at a level that is safely within your present capabilities. Then increase the intensity (overload) of the exercise regularly in small increments. Each individual adapts at his/her own rate, so you should not be discouraged if you do not progress as rapidly as someone else. The results of a programme of progressive resistance will depend upon three variables:

1. The amount of stress placed on the muscles;
2. The duration of the exercise period; and
3. The frequency of the exercise periods.

Widely separated or irregular practice periods should be avoided, but results are obtained when practice periods are evenly spaced to allow for good progression. For general fitness training, three days a week is adequate. Results will be more rapid if the exercises are not practised on succeeding days. Allow one day of rest between exercise days so the muscles of your body can recuperate. Do not train your body parts every day: your muscles must get rest and recovery in order to use the progression and overload principles.

Repetitions (reps) refer to the number of complete and continuous executions of an exercise. The term 1RM refers to the maximum amount of weight that can be lifted at one time. The resistance must be sufficiently large to demand greater-than-normal effort, but small enough to require a less than maximal effort.

Rep execution – the eccentric (lowering) phase of a lift – should be done slowly with good control; pause at the midpoint, then drive up as explosively as possible on the concentric (raising) phase. This strict downward control and explosive upward drive should be used on all lifts. The muscle, not gravity, should move the weight. Make every rep count – never bounce or jerk the weight. Have complete control of the weight throughout the full range of motion.

N.B. Emphasize strict control on the lowering phase.

Using this strict technique improves lifting discipline. Also, great strength and endurance is developed with fewer repetitions because of the slower lowering phase. The pause and explosive

## Safe and Successful Weight Training *continued*

drive in the raising phase work to develop fast twitch muscle fibres, improving speed and power.

A set refers to the number of repetitions of an exercise. If you press 100 pounds ten times, you have performed one set of ten repetitions. A short rest interval (one minute) should follow each set before attempting the next set. When you are able to do all sets of an exercise at a set weight, you should increase the resistance at the next workout. This upward progression stimulates the overload principle necessary to improve your body strength – any exercise that exceeds in intensity or duration the demands regularly made on the organism. Regardless of how much a muscle is used, it will not become stronger unless it is overloaded and made to overcome progressively increased resistance. To develop strength, overload can be established by increasing:

1. The load lifted;
2. The number of repetitions;
3. The speed of contraction;
4. The length of time a position is held; or
5. Any combination of 1–4.

Maximum muscular strength gains can be obtained from a heavy-resistance–low-repetition programme, while muscular endurance is more effectively achieved through a light-resistance–high-repetition programme.

*Fig. 91. A free-weights gym used by élite swimmers.*

| Reps | Multiplier | Reps | Multiplier |
|------|-----------|------|-----------|
| 1 | 1.00 | 11 | 0.723 |
| 2 | 0.943 | 12 | 0.703 |
| 3 | 0.906 | 13 | 0.688 |
| 4 | 0.881 | 14 | 0.675 |
| 5 | 0.856 | 15 | 0.662 |
| 6 | 0.831 | 16 | 0.650 |
| 7 | 0.807 | 17 | 0.638 |
| 8 | 0.786 | 18 | 0.627 |
| 9 | 0.765 | 19 | 0.616 |

If you know how many repetitions you can do for a certain weight, and you want to find out what the maximum should be for that exercise, divide the multiplier by the number of repetitions.

For example, you are working on a periodized programme, and you need to find percentages of your one-rep maximum to set up your weight-lifting routines. You don't have a spotter available to help you find a rep max on the exercise, but you do know you can just perform 12 good reps at 55kg.

55 divided by 0.703 = 78.

Your theoretical one-repetition maximum (1RM) should be around 78kg.

Fig. 92 1RM conversion table.

The following exercises and photographs are for swimmers in the 'Train to Compete' (T2C) and 'Train to Win' (T2W) phases of the LTAD model (Figs 12 and 15, *see* pages 26 and 31) and should not be performed without adequate experience, training background or appropriate supervision. A guide to safe and successful 'lifting' is provided.

The guidelines given in the box on pages 110–11 refer to something called 1RM, i.e. the amount of weight that can be lifted just once. It is the basis for all serious lifters to work out the loadings for their training, but it is *not* a useful tool for us to use in swimming. We are not particularly interested in testing what a swimmer's 1RM is because it is not as applicable to our needs. When in swimming do we ever do one maximal effort like a shot-putter or hammer thrower would do? But there is an easy conversion table that can be used to calculate training loadings just the same (Fig. 92).

When starting out on a new phase of training, swimmers should re-test their maximums and use this table to work out loadings based on their estimated 1RM. There are slight variations in whatever version of the chart you use and it should be used as a guide, not an absolute tool, but it is very useful and much more relevant to the needs of swimmers. Remember that Fig. 92 should be used for calculating the 1RM, not the ultimate training loads. It refers to your ability to perform maximally over the number of repetitions indicated, not what you should do for three sets of ten. Once the theoretical 1RM is known and the periodized programme is considered, then the actual training loadings can be calculated. Fig. 93 shows an early season week within the periodized programme for an Olympic-level swimmer previously shown (*see* Fig. 20, page 44).

The week is in the early season and is categorized as a 'medium' loading week. The 1RM for each exercise is shown in the final column and can be compared to the actual training load in the column before. The influence of the number of sets and repetitions on the loading can clearly be seen.

There is some debate about the value of fixed-resistance machines versus free weights. Many weight-training athletes (and strength and conditioning coaches), will attest that free weights are the be all and end all, while others will swear by machines. The truth is that both modes of training offer advantages to any and all weight-training individuals (although some research suggests that free weights promote quicker strength gains than machines). This can be attributed to many different factors,

| Rest Times | | | Mon 13 Oct | | | | |
|---|---|---|---|---|---|---|---|
| | | | Week 38 | | | | |
| | | | M - medium load | | | | |
| | | | 90 s/set & 90 s/ exercise | | | | |
| Session 1 | w-up | | training sets | | load | kg | 1RM |
| BB warm-up | | | | | | | |
| CG pull | 2x6 | 4 | x | 6 | M | 92 | 127 |
| Back squat | 1x10 | 3 | x | 8 | M | 82 | 120 |
| CG SLDL | | 3 | x | 10 | M | 56 | 88 |
| | | | | | | | |
| Bench press | 1x8 | 3 | x | 8 | M | 49 | 73 |
| Straight arm DB pullovers | | 3 | x | 8 | | | |
| BB rollouts | | 4 | x | 8 | | | |
| Prone bridge | | 4 | x | 30:10s | | | |
| | | | | | | | |
| Session 2 | w-up | | training sets | | load | kg | |
| BB warm-up | | | | | | | |
| Combination | | | | | | | |
| Hang clean (knee) | 2x6 | 1 | | | 32 | 55 | 84 |
| Push press | | 1 | 8 sets of 1 rep/exercise | | | | |
| Front squat | | 1 | | | | | |
| Push jerk | | 1 | | | | | |
| | | | | | | | |
| Lat pulldowns (cable) | | 3 | x | 8 | | | |
| Single arm DB row | | 3 | x | 8 | | | |
| Russian twists | | 4 | x | 8 | | | |
| Side bridge | | 2 | x | 30:10s | /side | | |
| | | | | | | | |
| Session 3 | w-up | | training sets | | load | kg | |
| BB warm-up | | | | | | | |
| Hang snatch (knee) | 2x6 | 4 | x | 6 | M | 46 | 63 |
| Overhead squat | 1x10 | 3 | x | 8 | M | 29 | 42 |
| SG SLDL | | 3 | x | 10 | M | 36 | 57 |
| | | | | | | | |
| Bench press | 1x8 | 3 | x | 8 | M | 49 | 73 |
| Single arm DB row | | 3 | x | 8 | | | |
| Plate walks | | 3 | x | 10 m | | | |
| Flat Crunch | | 3 | x | 10 | | | |

*Fig. 93. An early season weight training week.*

such as that free weights recruit more muscle groups and stabilizer muscles, and require more balance and co-ordination than do machines in the performance of exercise.

Free weights place resistance not only on the muscle that you are training, but on the stabilizer muscles that act to help stabilize your body (hold you in place) while you are exercising, and free weights also require you to balance the bar-bell or dumb-bells that you are training with. For example, when you perform the bench-press exercise with free weights, not only is your chest being trained, but the muscles that act to stabilize you and allow you to balance the weight as you are performing this exercise; your shoulders, triceps and upper back, to name but a few, also play a role. Comparatively when you bench press on a machine, the machine largely takes over the task of stabilizing you.

Free weights also provide more variation in the range of motion of a particular exercise, and more closely mimic natural body movements, thereby allowing your body to move through a more natural plane of motion as compared to that of a machine that is fixed and rigid, and only provides a range of motion through one specific path (typically a straight line or arc). In addition, free weights are the preferred mode of training for many of today's top body-builders and power-lifters, and no less an authority that Arnold Schwarzenegger has stated that he has 'always preferred free weights to machines in his training'.

Machines on the other hand also have many advantages. Most machines provide what is known as rotary and balanced resistance. Rotary resistance basically means that resistance will be placed on the muscle that you are training throughout the given exercise's full range of motion. For example in the bar-bell curl (free-weight exercise), your biceps have weight on them at the start position (bottom) but do not have weight on them at the end position (top). Comparatively with a machine curl, weight is placed on your biceps throughout the entire range of motion of this exercise, both at the bottom and the top position, providing a superior form of stress on your working muscles by means of continuous tension and peak contraction.

Balanced resistance means that the stress placed on your muscle by the given exercise is balanced throughout that exercise's full range of motion, and will compensate for naturally strong and weak portions of the arc (range of motion) for each movement (exercise). Again, in the case of the bar-bell curl (free-weight exercise), your biceps are much stronger at the starting position (bottom), than in the mid-range position (middle) of this exercise. So, for the bar-bell curl, it will be easier to perform the motion at the starting position (bottom) than to perform it in the mid-range position. With a machine curl, resistance is balanced by the machine and the weight will be functionally heavier at the starting position (bottom) of the curl. In addition, machines are ideal for people that are training alone in that they have built-in safety features, such as foot pedals and pins, and do not require a spotter. Furthermore, machines are typically used by individuals who are rehabilitating injuries because they specifically isolate certain muscle groups and provide a more controlled range of motion.

While both modes of training – free weights and machines – each have their unique advantages in the realms of weight training, it is important to realize that neither mode is superior to the other. The best approach to follow when weight training is to incorporate both modes of training into your training programme. Doing so will ensure that you are training your muscles as fully and completely as possible, thereby deriving the advantages of each training mode. In addition, you will provide the necessary variety to your training, which is crucial in order to continuously produce results to your physique, and to prevent boredom and burn-out in your training.

## Weight-Training Exercises

These exercises are for experienced swimmers with a good background of land training and an individualized programme of conditioning. There are not as many illustrations here as there are in some other sections of the book, and anyone requiring more information should seek out a qualified strength and conditioning coach. The exercise descriptions should give a basic indication of the movement patterns.

## Dumb-Bell Press

Lie on the bench holding two dumb-bells, face up. Lower each weight until level with the chest then return. On the up phase, rotate the shoulders externally. At the bottom the thumbs point inwards. At the top, thumbs point behind the head. At the low point the elbows should be at 90 degrees, in line with the shoulders. This exercise is shown in Fig. 62 and can be performed on a bench or on the Swiss ball, as illustrated.

## Dumb-Bell Single-Arm Row

With the left hand and left knee on a bench, support the body so the back is flat. The right hand holds a dumb-bell at arm's length. The dumb-bell is lifted to the armpit. Pull the elbow as high as possible. Do not rotate the torso. Repeat on the right side.

## Dumb-Bell Triceps Extension

Lie on a bench holding two dumb-bells, face down. The whole body is held taut with both arms at the side. The elbows are now extended as the shoulders lift to simulate the last part of the butterfly or front crawl stroke. This can be done with single alternate arms or both arms together.

## Olympic Bar Clean

Stand over the bar-bell with the balls of the feet positioned under the bar, slightly wider apart than hip width. Squat down and grip the bar with an overhand grip slightly wider than shoulder width. Position the shoulders over the bar with the back arched tightly. Arms are straight with elbows pointed along the bar. Pull the bar up off the floor by extending the hips and knees. As the bar reaches the knees, vigorously raise the shoulders while keeping the bar-bell close to the thighs. When the bar-bell passes mid-thigh, allow it to contact the thighs. Jump upward extending the body. Shrug the shoulders and pull the bar-bell upward with the arms allowing the elbows to flex out to the sides, keeping the bar close to the body. Aggressively pull the body under the bar, rotating the elbows around the bar. Catch the bar on the shoulders while moving into a squat position. Hitting the bottom of the squat, stand up immediately. To begin again, bend the knees slightly and lower bar-bell to mid-thigh position. Slowly lower bar with taut lower back and trunk close to vertical.

---

**Top Tip**

Do not jerk the weight from the floor; rise steadily, then accelerate. In the clean, the bar-bell is lifted from the floor to the shoulders. The lift is complete when the feet are in line and the bar is under control.

---

## Olympic Bar Hang Clean

Stand with bar-bell with overhand grip slightly wider than shoulder width. Bend knees and hips so bar-bell touches mid-thigh; shoulders are over the bar and the back is arched. Arms are straight with elbows pointed along the bar. Jump upwards extending the body. Shrug the shoulders and pull the bar-bell upward with the arms allowing the elbows to flex out to the sides, keeping the bar close to the body. Aggressively pull the body under the bar, rotating the elbows around the bar. Catch the bar on the shoulders while moving into a squat position. Hitting the bottom of the squat, stand up immediately. To begin again, bend the knees slightly and lower bar-bell to mid-thigh position. Pull bar up in a straight path keeping bar close to body.

## Olympic Bar Squat

The feet are hip-width apart, toes pointing slightly outwards. The bar is held behind the head, resting on the upper back/shoulders. Whilst holding a normal back position, the knees and hips are first flexed to lower the body, then extended to return it to the start.

*Olympic Bar Overhead Squat (Fig. 94)*
Snatch or hang snatch bar-bell overhead with a very wide overhand grip. Position toes outward with wide stance. Maintain bar behind head with arms extended. Descend until knees and hips are fully bent or until thighs are just past parallel to floor. Knees travel in

*Fig. 94. Olympic bar overhead squat.*

direction of toes. Extend knees and hips until legs are straight. Return and repeat.

| **Top Tip** |
| --- |
| Keep head forward, back straight and feet flat on the floor, with equal distribution of weight through forefoot and heel. |

*Bench Press (Machine or Free Weight)*
Lie supine on bench with upper chest under bar. Grasp bar with a wide oblique overhand grip. Lower weight to upper chest. Press bar until arms are extended. Repeat.

*Roll-Outs (Bar or Dumb-Bells) (Fig. 95)*
Similar to the Swiss-ball exercise demonstrated in Fig. 60 (*see* page 86), the roll-outs with a bar or bar-bell are performed with maximum control of the trunk. Shown in Fig. 95 it is essential that alignment and control are maintained throughout. This is an advanced exercise and therefore should be used only by very experienced swimmers.

*Machine Seated Row*
Sit tall on the seat and grasp the handles in an over-grasp. Pull strongly with both hands. Squeeze the scapulae together at the end of the movement.

*Machine Lat Pull-Down*
Sit tall on the seat and grasp the bar at just wider than shoulder width. Leading with the elbows pull the bar down to just under the chin. Control the return. Do not lean back and use your bodyweight to bring the stack up.

*Machine Incline Pull-Down (Fig. 96)*
Start in a standing position, keeping the head and spine in alignment. Pull the stack down towards the knees with the elbows kept high. (If you cannot keep the alignment, lower the weight.)

*Fig. 95. Roll-outs (bar or dumb-bells).*

## LAND TRAINING 'AT HOME'

Most committed swimmers will do some type of 'extra' training at home, whether it be stretching, watching videos or even some conditioning work. In the absence of any expensive or complex equipment, the training that swimmers will most commonly do is abdominal work. In fact most of the Swiss-ball exercises shown earlier can be done at home, but the traditional '500 sit-ups a day' routine is not such a bad idea at all. This does not have to be prescribed by the coach, but if swimmers are going to do additional work it is best performed correctly. The following exercises can be done on a daily basis either on your own, or as part of a 'mini' circuit designed by the swimmer, from the SwimSkills level onwards.

*Fig. 96. Machine incline pull-down.*

## Sit-Up Progressions

*Sit-Ups with Bent Knees (Fig. 97)*
1. Bottom to your heels as close as you can.
2. Hands together behind your head.
3. Elbows forward.
4. Hollow in the chest.
5. Back on the floor (there should not be any space/holes between your back and the floor).

The sit-ups should be like a roll-up. You should roll all the way up until your chest touches your knees. On the way down you unroll. For example: imagine yourself rolling up a newspaper and then unrolling it.

On the way up, you go fast!

On the way down, you go slow!

There should not be any sound as you reach the floor. Do not drop to the floor hard. When this exercise becomes easy you will need to increase speed and repetitions. A variation to this exercise can be added to the roll-down – a hollow hold with bent knees. At the end of the roll-down, the swimmer can stop/pause and hold their body close to the ground. The back should not touch the ground. First you can do this with bent arms. Then you can try with straight arms. Stretch tall making sure there are no holes between the neck, head and arms.

*Twist/Turn Sit-Ups (Fig. 98)*
Both bent-knee and straight-leg sit-ups can be done with a turn/twist at the top of the sit-up. Remember to follow the steps above for bent knee sit-ups.

*Fig. 97. Sit-ups with bent knees.*

*Fig. 98. Twist/turn sit-ups.*

- Do not arch on the way up and down.
- Roll and unroll.
- The twist/turn is done at the end/top of the sit-up. Then roll down.

*Twist/Turn in the Hollow Position (Left and Right)*

When hollow holds become easy, you can add a twist/turn in the hollow-hold position (left

Fig. 99. 'V' sit-ups.

and right). It is important to hold the body in this hollow position and not to arch in the lower back or chest.

### 'V' Sit-Ups (Fig. 99)

Lie down straight on the floor. The lower back should be on the floor. Your arms should be stretching tall on the floor without any holes between your arms and head. When you begin the exercise, be sure to keep the arms stretching behind the ears.

Fold the body in half to form a V, bringing both halves of the V together at the same time – as a book in your hand would fold. At the end of the sit-up you should be reaching past your toes, with your head, chest and stomach close to the legs.

This exercise should be done quickly up and quickly down. At the end of the required numbers, you should hold the last V position for 10 seconds. This exercise should also be done quietly – no noise and no drops.

*Fig. 100. Crunches.*

*Crunches (Fig. 100)*
Start with the feet off the ground and bring the head towards the knees. Control the descent and maintain tension in the abdominals throughout.

**Body-Weight Exercises**

*Press-Up (Knees) (Fig. 101)*
The knees are positioned on the floor behind the hips; the hands are under the shoulders and the back is flat to make a triangular shape. Keep the movements smooth and slow. Lower the chin to the floor and return.

*Press-Up (Full) (Fig. 102)*
With the hands at shoulder width and the body in complete tension, lower the chin to the floor and return. Straighten the elbows but do not lock them. Keep the movements smooth and slow.

*Fig. 101. Press-up (knees).*

*Fig. 102. Press-up (full).*

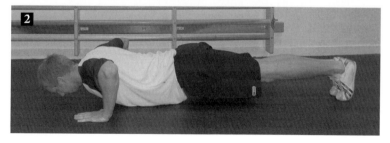

*Fig. 103. Reverse press-up (dips).*

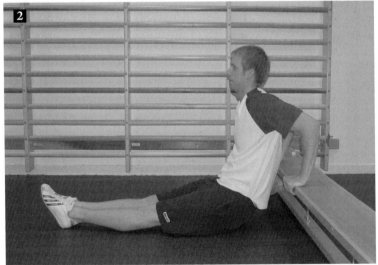

*Reverse Press-Up (Dips) (Fig. 103)*

Using a bench for stability, position the hands behind the back on the bench; straighten the legs out in front. Lower the body by bending the arms, then push the body back to the starting position. A great workout for the triceps.

*Squat Jump (Fig. 104)*

Keeping the ankles, knees, hips and shoulders in alignment, perform squat jumps straight up in the air. If starting with one foot in front of the other, remember to alternate the front foot each time you jump.

*Fig. 104. Squat jump.*

*Squat Thrust (Fig. 105)*
Start in the press-up bridge position and thrust the feet and knees forwards between the arms. Straighten the legs out each time they push back.

*Rebound Jump (Fig. 106)*
Start in a position close to the wall with the arms straight above the head, hands just touching the wall. Continuously jump and rebound up and down just using the calf and ankle muscles. Great for turns!

**Flexibility**

Flexibility is the range of motion (ROM) in a joint or combination of joints. The main purpose of flexibility is to help prevent injuries. Adequate cool-down, such as flexibility exercises, help to prevent strains, muscle

*Fig. 105. Squat thrust.*

*Fig. 106.
Rebound jump.*

tears and soreness that normally will occur if a swimmer does not stretch. Furthermore, poor flexibility will have a detrimental effect on speed, since the muscles have to work harder to bring about a maximum stroke length. This extra work results in a greater loss of energy and will obviously hinder your performance in the pool. By increasing the flexibility of the ankles, hips, trunk and shoulder, greater speed can be achieved, as well as saving a great deal of energy; allowing you to train harder and longer.

The main purpose of a warm-up is to raise both the general body and the deep-muscle temperatures and to stretch the ligaments in order to permit greater flexibility. For this reason, the dynamic warm-up routine explained previously is preferred to the static-stretching exercises that are described in this section; however, these should form the basis of an effective post-swim routine.

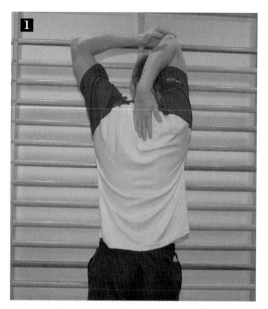

*Fig. 107. Triceps stretch.*

*Fig. 108. Chest and shoulders stretch.*

*Fig. 109. Big circles.*

Fig. 110. Hanging hamstring stretch.

This flexibility programme takes about ten minutes and can easily be performed after leaving the pool. Some individuals need considerably more time than this to feel stretched and recovered, and should, by all means, put in the extra time, if required. You do not have to do all of the stretches illustrated here. Create your own programme from these exercises and others that can be done to form a personal stretching routine that you own and take responsibility for. Take the time to enjoy your flexibility programme rather than going into it with the attitude of 'I need to hurry up and get this over with'. Use this time to relax your mind and muscles, and to focus in on recovering from the just-completed session. It is also a great time to interact with other swimmers and your coach.

A stretch for the triceps and the top of the shoulder, pull the elbow behind the head for a 10 seconds stretch for each arm (Fig. 107).

With interlaced fingers, turn the elbows in while inhaling and extending the chest up and

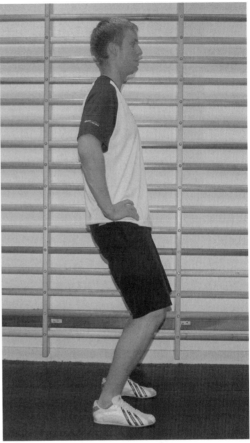

Fig. 111. Quarter-squat stretch.

out as you lift up your arms (Fig. 108). Hold this for 15 seconds.

With your hands locked over your head, bend at the waist and try to pull your hand to the floor, keeping your arms behind your head. Hold this for 10 seconds each side (Fig. 109).

From a standing position with feet about shoulder-width apart, bend forward from the waist letting your neck and arms relax. Go to the point where you feel a slight stretch and let the weight of the upper body do the stretching (Fig. 110). Concentrate on relaxing the back and the hamstrings. *Do not bounce* – hold this

*Fig. 112. Sitting-hamstring stretch #1.*

*Fig. 113. Sitting-hamstring stretch #2.*

*Fig. 114. Sitting-hamstring stretch #3.*

*Fig. 115. Spinal-twist stretch #1.*

stretch for 30 seconds. Bend the knees before standing back up.

The quarter squat is designed with the idea of tensing the quads as the hamstrings relax (Fig. 111). Hold this for 20 seconds and then go back to the hamstring stretch (Fig. 110). After holding the quarter-squat position, go back to stretching the hamstrings – this time hold the stretch for 25 seconds, still concentrating on relaxing the muscle being stretched while keeping knees locked. Remember – concentrate on relaxing the muscle being stretched. Do not bounce; keep even pressure on the stretch at all times.

Sit down with your legs straight and heels between 15 and 20cm (6 and 8in) apart. Reach down to the ankles or the toes, feeling the stretch just behind the knees (Fig. 112) or, if your back is tight, you will also feel the stretch across the back. For the more flexible individuals, extra stretch can be attained by pointing the toes back toward the head (Fig. 113), by lifting the head and putting the chest down on the knees, or by using both of these techniques. If your flexibility is at a

point where you cannot reach down to grasp the toes or the ankles, simply hook a towel over your feet and, as you gain in flexibility, you will be able to grasp further and further down the towel until you are able to reach the toes or ankles (Fig. 114). Hold this stretch for 20 seconds. Again, keep the knees locked.

The spinal-twist stretch (Fig 115) is very good for the muscles along the spine and each side of the hips, as well as the arms. It will help you turn to look behind you without having to turn your whole body. Starting with your legs straight, take the left leg and cross it over the right leg and place the left foot flat on the ground. With your right arm reach around your bent leg as if you were trying to grab your left hip. Take your left arm and put it directly behind you as you slowly turn your head, sit up straight and look over your left shoulder. Hold this stretch for 10 seconds and then cross the right leg over the left leg and hold that stretch for 10 seconds. The spinal twist #2, shown in Fig. 116, is for those who cannot perform the twist with a straight bottom leg.

Fig. 116. Spinal-twist stretch #2.

Fig. 117. Groin stretch.

The stretch shown in Fig. 117 is for stretching the groin area, and for some it may also stretch the back. Put the soles of your feet together and grab around your toes, gently pulling yourself forward until you feel a good stretch in the groin. Notice the elbows are outside the knees giving stability to the stretch.

Remember – do not bounce on your stretches. Keep even pressure on the stretch at all times.

Cradling the leg around the knee and the ankle, pull the leg as one unit up to the chest (Fig. 118). Do not try to force the knee to your chest – relaxation in this stretch will help

Fig. 118. Adductor stretch.

*Fig. 119. Quad stretch.*

tremendously. If this position does not give you a good stretch, lie back and stretch. Hold this stretch for 20 seconds and then move to the next exercise.

Lie on your side and stretch the leg you have just been stretching in the cradle stretch. Grab the ankle of the leg you are going to stretch and slowly move your hips forward (Fig. 119). Concentrate on the stretch that you get in the quadriceps. Hold this stretch for 10 seconds and then move on. This next stretch is for your calves. Place your hands directly in front of you and place your feet flat on the ground. Concentrate on your calves and hold for 20 seconds. For this stretch you straighten the leg that we were stretching before and bend the other leg in with the sole of the foot on the thigh of the straight leg. From this position, bend forward at the waist toward the foot of the straight leg. It is very important in this stretch that you keep your leg straight and your toe pointed up (Fig. 120). Hold this stretch for 30 seconds.

*Fig. 120. Sitting single-hamstring stretch #1.*

*Fig. 121. Spinal mobility.*

*Fig. 122. Lower-back stretch.*

Now repeat these three stretches for the prescribed amount of time for the other leg. Whether you are right- or left-handed, stretch the side that is the tightest of the two first, since you will have a natural tendency to spend more time on the first part of your stretching programme.

In a sitting position with your chin tucked on your chest, pull your knees to your chest and gently roll up and down your spine (Fig. 121). Try to roll as evenly and controlled as possible between four to eight times or until you feel your back begin to limber up. On the last roll backward, keep going back and over with the feet, ending up in a stretch (Fig. 122). In this stretch, your feet and legs are over your head with your hands at your hips for support and control of the stretch. Do not hold your breath or stretch in a position that cuts off your supply of air. Once you find a comfortable position, relax. Hold this for 20 seconds.

From this, with the legs overhead, put your hands behind your knees and keep your legs bent as you roll down slowly. Roll vertebra by vertebra, while you keep you head on the ground – this takes 10–15 seconds.

Extend your arms overhead and your legs straight out, pointing your toes and reaching as far as you can (Fig. 123). For a diagonal stretch, point the fingers of the right hand and the toes of the left foot and hold. Then point the left hand and the right foot and hold. Hold for 5 seconds and then relax completely.

Hold the left leg just below the knee and pull it toward your chest (Fig. 124). Keep the back of your head down and then slowly

*Fig. 123. Elongation stretch.*

*Fig. 124. Buttock stretch.*

Fig. 125. Lower back and buttock stretch.

bring your head up toward your bent knee. Hold this stretch for 10 seconds.

From here gently bend the leg that you were stretching over the leg that was straight (Fig. 125). Look to the opposite shoulder (down the arm that is extended). Hold for 20 seconds.

Repeat these for the other leg, hip, back, upper back and shoulder. These stretches will also stretch the hamstring.

Fig. 126 (a). Sitting single-hamstring stretch #1.

*Fig. 126 (b). Sitting single-hamstring stretch #2.*

Sit up with your legs spread-eagled as wide as they will go and as you slowly bend forward to stretch rotate your hips forward also (Fig. 126 (a)). Keep the legs straight and your toes pointed up. If possible hold your hands out in front while holding a comfortable relaxed position for the stretch. Hold this portion of the stretch for 20 seconds.

From the stretch to the middle you move to one leg to stretch the hamstring (Fig. 126 (b)). Again, keep your head forward and your back straight as you hold this stretch for 20 seconds before stretching the other leg for 20 seconds.

Put the soles of the feet together and grab around your toes as you gently pull yourself forward. Hold for 20 seconds.

Saigon squat with your feet flat and toes pointed out at a 45-degree angle with heels 10–30cm (4–12in) apart, depending on your flexibility (Fig. 127). This stretches the front

*Fig. 127. Saigon-squat stretch.*

135

*Fig. 128. Hip-flexor stretch.*

part of the lower legs, the knees, back, ankles, Achilles tendons and deep groin. Hold for 10 seconds.

Place your foot flat in front of you with the knee behind you on the floor and slowly extend out over the toe with the back knee keeping contact with the ground (Fig. 128). To intensify the stretch and to stretch more of the groin area, straighten out the back leg and gently lower your upper body to the inside of the knee of the forward leg. Use your hands for balance. The feeling of the stretch will be in the groin, front of the hip, hamstrings and calf.

---

**Top Tip**

Do all stretches in a controlled fashion – do not bounce! Concentrate on relaxing the muscle groups being stretched.

---

# CHAPTER 4

# Special Considerations

## CHILDREN

There is a popular notion that young children (i.e. under 12 years) cannot benefit from appropriate land-based conditioning programmes. This has been widely refuted by various research studies world-wide and is not the view of the prestigious American College of Sports Medicine (ACSM) who state that:

> ...contrary to the traditional belief that strength training is dangerous for children or that it could lead to bone plate disturbances, the ACSM contends that strength training can be a safe and effective activity for this age group, provided that the program is properly designed and competently supervised. It must be emphasized, however, that strength training is a specialized form of physical conditioning distinct from the competitive sports of weightlifting and powerlifting, in which individuals attempt to lift maximal amounts of weight in competition.

Providing that the basic components of the programme includes flexibility, general body conditioning and movement co-ordination, there is no lower age-limit to training. Simple equipment – such as skipping ropes, stretchcords, hand-held weights, medicine balls and Swiss balls – are commonly added to basic exercise movements. Supervised sessions of 20–30 minutes that are appropriate to the child's level of development can provide a valuable addition to the swimming programme and provide some fun along the way.

Prior to puberty, exercise sessions should progressively increase in intensity, frequency and complexity. The LTAD model used for swimmers includes core strength and range of movement exercises, in addition to the development of technical swimming skills. The overall objective is an even and balanced development of all muscle groups used in swimming. Many young swimmers will achieve these strength goals by participating in other sports programmes (in addition to swim training) during the year. Gymnastics is especially useful. It should be remembered, however, that young swimmers of a similar age will progress in their strength development at different rates.

Learning 'how' to exercise is a major objective during the pre-maturation years. Coaches should insist upon an appropriate warm-up, correct exercise technique and, even at this stage, proper integration of land-based exercises with the swimming programme, i.e. when, how often, and what the effects on pool work will be. Speed of movement in performing the various exercises can be progressively increased once correct technique is being maintained. Body weight and simple resistance exercises are usually performed in 'sets' (i.e. multiple repetitions) and then multiple sets are progressively added. Land-based exercises are generally used for muscle 'strength-endurance' training. This complements the muscle-endurance improvements that result from swimming training alone.

The aim is to keep the exercise programme simple, yet include enough variety to maintain interest and enthusiasm. As has already been established, all land-based exercise must fit within the overall training demands of the swimming programme. When young swimmers are ready to handle more complex gym routines, they usually graduate to 'circuit training' methods. As explained in Chapter 3, resistance, rest and repetitions are used to manipulate the relative characteristics of the exercise programme in circuit training, and this form of training is commonly and successfully used with age-group swimmers across the world, every week.

Advanced strength-training programmes feature more specialized exercises to suit the swimmer's individual needs. However, all swimmers should be assessed on a regular basis to determine their relative strength deficiencies and specific exercise requirements. Strength training should always be integrated into the swimming programme so that overall swimming performance is enhanced. A 'strong' swimmer who does not swim fast has not trained effectively in both pool and gym. As with most other contentious issues in training, there are powerful arguments in favour of, and against, aspects of land training for young swimmers. An excellent aphorism used by US expert Vern Gambetta in setting out the issues is: 'It's not the sport that determines the training process; it is the developmental stage of the child.'

Others assert that pre-pubertal dedicated strength activities are inappropriate and unjustified. They claim that pre-pubertal children do not have high enough levels of testosterone to respond markedly to strength training other than that gained through learning the skill of the exercise. This is in marked contrast to the empirical research evidence, which although recommending a conservative approach to pre-adolescent strength training, does not find any great injury risk with this form of training under appropriate instruction. Several studies in the 1980s demonstrated that pre-pubescent boys and girls can participate safely in resistance training with marked strength gains.

As evidenced by their strong opposition to land training for swimmers, Rushall and Pyke have further views on the use of strength training for children (Rushall and Pyke, 1990, p. 37):

> Thus, there is likely to be no carry-over of strength exercise training effects to swimming performances. Training during the adolescent growth spurt would seem to be the most advantageous time to perform strength/ power/auxiliary training. Growth will be directed toward the training stimulation. Once athletes mature and stop growing, stimulating strength/power training needs only to be of a predominantly maintenance form. Since growth has stopped adaptability will be very limited. If strength training is performed excessively, then muscle hypertrophy occurs. Increased muscle mass increases the specific density of the swimmer causing him/her to settle deeper in the water. The increased resistance from the outcome would be detrimental to swimming efficiency.

There may a confusion of two different arguments at play here. Rushall and Pyke are arch-critics of the use of land training in swimming, so will clearly not support the use of weight training for younger athletes, where there are many other arguments present, both ethical and developmental. A helpful clarification to their contention would be to define exactly what they mean by 'strength/power/auxiliary' training, since they would appear to be distinctly different training methods altogether and may have no absolute 'carry-over' value to performance, but could still contribute to general conditioning and athletic ability.

Despite the paucity of research evidence about the transfer effects of land training to swimming performance (at any age), no less an authority than the National Strength and Conditioning Association (NSCA; *see* Useful Addresses) does support the use of appropriate strength- and resistance-training programmes with young athletes with the following position statement:

- A properly designed and supervised resistance training program is safe for children.
- A properly designed and supervised resistance training program can increase the strength of children.
- A properly designed and supervised resistance training program can help to enhance the motor fitness skills and sports performance of children.
- A properly designed and supervised resistance training program can help to prevent injuries in youth sports and recreational activities.
- A properly designed and supervised resistance training program can help to improve the psychosocial well-being of children.
- A properly designed and supervised resistance training program can enhance the overall health of children.

Children and adolescents need to participate regularly in physical activities that enhance and maintain cardiovascular and musculoskeletal health. While boys and girls have traditionally been encouraged to participate in aerobic training and strength-building activities, a growing number of children and adolescents are experiencing the benefits of plyometric training. Plyometrics, as discussed in Chapter 3, refers to exercises that link strength with speed of movement to produce power, and were first known simply as 'jump training'. Previously thought of as a method of conditioning reserved for adult athletes, plyometric training is – contends the American College of Sports Medicine (ACSM) – a safe, beneficial and fun activity for children and adolescents provided that the programme is properly designed and supervised.

To recap, plyometric training conditions the body through dynamic, resistance exercises. This type of training typically includes hops and jumps and medicine-ball throws that exploit the muscles' cycle of lengthening and shortening to increase muscle power. Plyometric exercises start with a rapid stretch of a muscle (eccentric phase) and are followed by a rapid shortening of the same muscle (concentric phase). With plyometric training, the nervous system is conditioned to react more quickly to the stretch–shortening cycle.

This type of training is thought to enhance a child's ability to increase speed of movement and improve power production. Regular participation in a plyometric training programme may also help to strengthen bone and facilitate weight control. Furthermore, plyometric training performed during the pre-season phase of swimming training may decrease the risk of sports-related injuries. There are literally dozens of plyometric exercises for the upper and lower body, ranging from low-intensity double leg hops to high-intensity drills such as combined jumps and throws. Although these are typically associated with plyometric training for the mature athlete, common games and activities such as hopping, skipping and star jumps can also be characterized as plyometrics because every time the feet make contact with the ground the quadriceps are subjected to the stretch–shortening cycle. In fact, plyometrics are a natural part of most movements, as evidenced by the jumping, hopping and skipping seen in any school playground.

With qualified coaching and instruction appropriate to age, plyometric training can be a safe, effective and fun method of conditioning for young swimmers. However, there is the potential for injury to occur if the intensity and volume of the training programme exceeds the abilities of the participants. Children and adolescents should develop an adequate baseline of strength before participating in a plyometric training programme, or they should simply begin plyometric training with lower intensity drills and gradually progress to higher intensity drills over time.

Although additional empirical studies are needed to determine the most effective plyometric training programme for children and adolescents, it seems reasonable to begin with one to three sets of six to ten repetitions on one upper-body exercise (e.g. medicine ball chest pass with a one-kilogram ball) and one lower-body exercise (e.g. double leg hop) twice per week on non-consecutive days. If multiple sets are performed, participants must be provided with adequate rest and recovery between sets (e.g. two to four minutes) in order to replenish the energy necessary to perform the next series of repetitions with the same intensity. Unlike traditional strength-training exercises, plyometric exercises are performed quickly and explosively. Plyometric exercises may be introduced into the warm-up period, e.g. skipping, or incorporated into group game activities, which most children will do naturally anyway.

Depending upon individual needs and goals, the plyometric training programme can progress to include multiple jumps, single leg hops and throws using lightweight medicine balls. Modifying the programme over time will help to optimize gains and prevent over-training. Age-group swimmers should be provided with specific information on proper exercise technique, rate of progression and safe training procedures (e.g. warm-up and cool-down). Also, they must wear supportive footwear (not the trendy flat-soled shoes favoured by so many young swimmers, and certainly not bare feet) and plyometric exercises should be performed on surfaces with some resilience, ideally a sprung wooden floor or a thin mat. Plyometrics are not intended to be a stand-alone exercise programme and should be incorporated into a well-designed overall conditioning programme that also includes strength, endurance, flexibility and agility training.

Plyometric training may not only make swimmers faster and more powerful but offer observable general health benefits to young people. The contention that plyometrics are inappropriate for boys and girls is not consistent with the needs of children and teenagers or their physical abilities. Plyometric training is a safe, worthwhile and fun method of conditioning for children and adolescents, if age-appropriate guidelines are followed, qualified instruction is available, and individual concerns are addressed.

Preparation of young swimmers is often referred to as 'an easy task' and at one level it is. Swimmers will naturally grow and mature physically and if they are 'competitive' to begin with, the job of the coach is made considerably easier. But there is much more to the effective development of young swimmers than this, quite apart from the technical objectives of building sound foundations for stroke developments in later years; there is still much for the coach to do in a physical sense that can influence how close a swimmer can come to fulfilling their potential throughout their career. For some assistance, we need look no further again than the sport of gymnastics.

It is no coincidence that some of the best swimmers that I have coached have had a background in gymnastics as youngsters and more (enlightened) swimming coaches are turning to their colleagues in this sport for help with the basics of movement and conditioning. I am not advocating that swimmers attempt to become gymnasts (although experience would show that this is not necessarily a terribly bad thing), merely that developing some gymnastic skills can have tremendous carry-over benefits to skill development and physiological conditioning for swimming. Fig. 129 shows a variety of themes and activities as part of an 'early' gymnastics development programme. At the very least an emphasis on the upper half of this diagram would be a good starting point for land-training content with younger age-group swimmers (7–11 years).

Gymnastics skills begin with fitness characteristics. If the young swimmer is not fit enough (i.e. strong, flexible, etc.), skill learning will be impossible. Of course, the swimmer cannot just condition and not practise skills. Skill practice should focus newly acquired fitness (e.g. strength and flexibility) in skill learning so that the fitness quality is focused specifically at these gymnastics skills. Following fitness, the swimmer should understand and be able to achieve the necessary body positions. In rolling, the coach should emphasize methods to clear the head and methods of making the roll smooth. Clearing the head may require considerable upper-body strength. Performing a smooth roll (i.e. not bumpy) requires that the swimmer's body moves smoothly from one contact point to the next (i.e. from shoulders to back to hips to feet). Upright balance and locomotion involves body shapes and simple movements. Upright balance, of course, does not involve being inverted. The swimmer learns about body shapes and body control while trying to hold unusual body positions in static and in upright locomotion. The swimmer should be instructed in appropriate body positions and postures. When the swimmer is asked to hold a balance position for a period of time or during a movement, the posture and position often deteriorate. Coaches should monitor the swimmer's body positions so that poor postures are identified early and the swimmer becomes able to identify and adopt specific body positions while moving.

Inverted-balance skills require a clear understanding of body positions while upright. Inverted skills place a great deal of stress on body positions and postures due to the disorienting influence of being upside-down. Because the acquisition of inverted-balance skills is difficult, the swimmer should be exposed to a number of different types of inverted balances. For example, there are many versions of headstands that can be used to help the swimmer learn about body position and postures while inverted. If headstands become too easy, then the swimmer can progress to forearm stands and handstands (*see* Fig. 8, page 18). Gymnasts are required to move into and from inverted positions, most commonly handstands, from all directions. Inverted-balance skills allow the swimmer to learn about movements into and out of upside-down positions in relatively slow and controllable ways. Again, coaches should emphasize sound body positions and postures at all points of the movement.

The wheel shown in Fig. 129 is a model of gymnastics instruction that establishes a general direction for instruction while allowing some freedom in actual skill selection. The curriculum wheel is an attempt to be simultaneously prescriptive and open-ended, to acknowledge an overall direction of instruction while incorporating individual learning paths. More information can be obtained from your local gymnastics club (*see* Useful Addresses for general contact details).

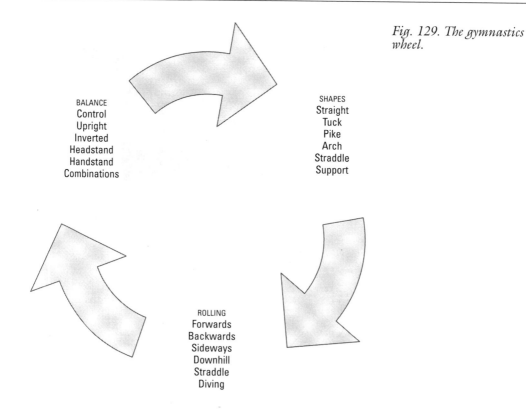

*Fig. 129. The gymnastics wheel.*

BALANCE
Control
Upright
Inverted
Headstand
Handstand
Combinations

SHAPES
Straight
Tuck
Pike
Arch
Straddle
Support

ROLLING
Forwards
Backwards
Sideways
Downhill
Straddle
Diving

## GENDER DIFFERENCES IN THE PLANNING OF LAND TRAINING

Although not necessarily a sport similar in either training or competition habits to swimming, gymnastics has many other parallels with swimming. Gymnasts, like swimmers, begin training at an early age. They also have a tradition of intensive training from this early specialization. Additionally, there is some evidence in swimming and gymnastics, of a marked reluctance by female competitors to undertake strength training. Coaches interviewed by the author in a research study were not specific in their comments about individualizing land training for girls, but they did give some examples of a different approach to the planning of workloads. My own coaching experience supports this evidence and suggests that there is still a significant aversion to weight training by some female swimmers. Taking a brief look at this particular issue, there are some lessons to be learned.

Gymnasts must remain on the lean side of lean to be effective competitors at the highest level. Not surprisingly, concern about excess body weight is very common. Female gymnasts and their coaches are therefore reluctant to use weight training, in spite of evidence of the benefits of weight training for sports requiring strength. Their concern is that the gymnast will develop excessive body and muscle mass and thus become too heavy to perform effectively. Gymnasts and other athletes who must move their body weight as the primary resistance, need to train for strength relative to body mass rather than absolute strength. As the gymnast matures, she is likely to gain absolute strength but lose relative strength as her body mass increases. Female gymnasts can increase reliance on motor skills to compensate for a decline in relative strength, but strength training aimed at increasing relative strength is another important approach.

While some gymnastics coaches are reluctant to prescribe weight training, most include strength training in the form of repetitions of strength-oriented gymnastics skills. Many gymnastics skills have a large strength component, so separating the skill performance from strength training is somewhat arbitrary. Most gymnastics coaches would agree that development of strength through repetition of gymnastics skills is appropriate. However, skills at the élite level are becoming ever more difficult, and extra time for training is at a premium. It is suggested that weight training may be orthopaedically less demanding than extra skill repetitions and require less time for these gymnasts.

There is no suggestion that female swimmers should follow this in totality, but with the average age of competitors rising every year, there may be some value in adopting a more balanced approach to training, both in and out of the pool, to safeguard longevity in the sport and avoid over-use injuries from excessive high-resistance swimming. Interesting footnotes to this point are the views of former World Record Holder Zoe Baker (aged 30) (BBCi, 2003):

Swimming training is becoming more and more similar to athletics training. Coaches have realized that fitness work should not just be done in the water. We do a lot of dry-land training as well and I can be seen doing weights and gym work outs all the time. There's no point just swimming 100 kilometres a week when it is actually more beneficial to do some running here and there. If someone watched us training they probably would not think it was that different to the way Linford Christie or Colin Jackson might train.

The fact that Baker swims in a 'power'-dominated event (50m breaststroke) may have something to do with her views and training programme, but the point is well made and supports both the 'science' of those involved with the gymnasts and the 'practice' of swimming coaches. Another great advocate for female swimmers and land training is the fact that the British Swimming CD-ROM (produced by Henryk Lakomy and Bob Smith and referred to in Chapter 1 of this book) uses Ros Brett as the subject in the images. A diminutive, but powerful figure, Brett ably demonstrates the benefits of land training for all swimmers in a positive and accurate way.

## LAND TRAINING DURING TAPERING FOR COMPETITION

One of the most common discussion topics among swimming coaches is tapering for important competitions. The ultimate concept of tapering is a legacy of an outmoded training model that is gradually being replaced as coaches embrace periodized training principles. However, there still is a need for swimmers to recover from extensive periods of general and specific fatigue, so that all the body's resources can be applied to competitive events.

The coaching strategy of working athletes hard and keeping them fatigued for many months was shown to be useful in the days when training usually did not fully stimulate or tax the physical capacities of individuals. As 'hard work' seemed to pay off, coaches logically assumed that if hard work produced desirable results, more and harder work would produce even better results. In swimming, and indeed in sports in general, that approach has been taken to extremes and is no longer supported by research evidence or the practices of very successful coaches and athletes. The British swimming team (under the guidance of coach Bill Sweetenham) operate a strict set of guidelines for competition performances with targets set at 3, 2 or 1 per cent above life-time best according to training status, competition emphasis and cyclical planning. This ensures that even at their most tired, in the hardest phase of training, swimmers have to perform very close to their best. The underlying belief that has long been touted among swimming coaches is that although swimmers are always tired and training hard, and performances are not changing or are even getting worse, good things are still happening to them. That is a false belief. Better swimmers come from periodized programmes, with demonstrable training effects being derived from the judicious use of work and recovery throughout the year. However, there are still significant benefits to be gained from fine-tuning the preparation in the lead-up to the major competition(s) of the season, i.e. the tapering period.

There are two basic research findings that should govern the underlying considerations for developing a taper.

1. Many coaches fear a loss of conditioning and performance if training is reduced for a long period (at least two or three weeks) before a major competition. Research has clearly shown that physiological gains achieved through extensive training are retained, even when work volumes are reduced by more than one-half. For some capacities, such as strength, the volume can be reduced to one-tenth and the capacity level will still be retained. Even days off are helpful.
2. The major benefit from a taper is the recovery and restoration that it facilitates. The features that actually influence the competitive performance are the quality and type of training that has preceded the taper. A competitive performance is best considered to be an indication of the training programme that the athlete experienced, not some magical activity that occurred during the taper. The nature of long-term training governs the type and level of performance that will be exhibited in serious competitions. If that investment is not correct and ultimately specific, high-level performances will not ensue, no matter how effective the taper.

These two principles set the basic guidelines for tapering:

1. Allow rest and recovery to occur fully without confusing the procedure with a loss of conditioning; and
2. Perform specific performance tasks that will replicate the demands of the intended competitive effort.

A modern interpretation of why tapering works is that only neuromuscular and psychological factors recover, i.e. there is little or no change in physiological status. What happens in a taper is that neural and cognitive capacities increase in use efficiency. Strength and power (neuromuscular functions) increase markedly and the propelling efficiency of strokes (largely a cognitive recovery function) also increases. For these reasons, it is futile to attempt to get 'extra' physiological capacities during a taper. Its programming should allow neural and cognitive performance factors to recover and become more finely tuned.

Research at the International Centre for Aquatic Research (ICAR) has shown the maximum length of a taper to be three weeks, with the possibility of it being extended to four weeks. There are a number of factors that modify the actual length:

- There is considerable individuality in the tapering response. It should not be assumed that a planned taper will be appropriate for all swimmers. For those who recover very quickly during a 'group' taper it may be necessary to reinstitute several days of quality training to delay the peaked state. While that form of training is being followed by some, others might be working lightly, as their slower recovery occurs. To accommodate individuality, a coach must be prepared to offer varied programmes for at least subgroups of swimmers, so that peaked performances will occur according to the individual needs of athletes.
- The competitive schedule of the swimmer will also determine when a taper should start and what are programmed as training items. For a swimmer who will compete in the most important event on the fourth day of a championships, the taper should start later than one who has to compete on the first day. However, the opportunity to do controlled convenient swimming is rarely afforded at championship meets. Thus, even though it seems logical to delay the late-performing athlete's taper, the nature of the work that can be done over the crucial last three or four days at the competition site may require compromised planning. Usually, the commencement of the taper should be delayed even longer if quality work and volume cannot be fully exploited at the competitive arena because of the extended rest that will occur there.
- The length of time that a swimmer has been in hard training is proportional to the length of time allocated to a taper. When a season of training is uninterrupted, the taper will be longest. However, when interruptions occur – for example, a swimmer is selected for a trip abroad, goes on holiday or is injured or ill – the length of a taper should be affected. Generally it can

be assumed that the closer the interruption to a championship meet, the shorter will be the taper period.

After the recommended maximum of three weeks for a taper, performance potential gradually decreases due to the less than adequate volume of event-specific training. Performance standards can remain very high past the three-week period but the swimmer gradually loses important performance capacities.

> The general length of a taper should be three weeks, but certain events can intervene and warrant shortening its duration.

It is possible to extend the effects of a taper by alternating short bursts of intense training (actions that re-stimulate the specifically prepared physiological and bio-mechanical functions) with recovery. This occurs when there are a number of important swimming competitions in close proximity, e.g. in 2002 the Commonwealth Games in Manchester were followed within a month by the Pan Pacific Championships in Japan and the Australian Short Course Championships. Apart from coping with the demands of travelling across the globe, the swimmers who took part in all three competitions were able to sustain such a high level of performance that they were still breaking records on the final day of swimming in Melbourne. That demanding schedule of competitive experiences required at least maintenance physical training to occur in the intervening time period.

> Taper effects can be extended by the judicious use of quality training stimuli on a maintenance-training schedule.

The volume of work in a taper should be reduced to at least 60 per cent of that which existed during heavy training. However, for programmes that have had excessive volumes of training (e.g. eleven sessions per week, 12km per day) the reduction could be to a level even below this. The principle of individuality has to be considered as a major moderating variable for determining the appropriate length of the training-volume reduction. Higher volume training in the days immediately preceding an event may be detrimental to performance, while a slow decay in volume will have a beneficial effect on maximizing competition preparation.

Some form of consistent performance measurement on at least an alternate-day schedule can be performed without any undue effect on competition performances. Times should be expected to gradually improve as the taper progresses.

> For a taper, training volume should be reduced to 60 per cent of normal heavy training volume.

The nature of the volume-reduction should be by session. Eleven training sessions a week should gradually be reduced to about half this number. It is wrong to continue an excessive number of sessions while performing smaller training session loads, but the mistake of removing all morning sessions from the schedule should not be made. Swimmers need to be able to swim fast in both morning (heat) and evening (semi- or finals) races. Eliminating morning sessions would be a fundamental error in final preparations for a major meet. Some reasons why sessions should be reduced are:

- The sessions off allow for greater recovery and energy restoration;
- The added rest time allows stresses from sources other than swimming to be tolerated; and
- There is a greater potential for restorative sleep to occur.

> The number of training sessions should be reduced in a taper rather than reducing session loads.

The way the volume decrease should occur is not clear from the research or from the practice of successful coaches. Neither a stepwise nor a sudden decrease in volume appears to be any better than the other. It is suggested that tapering really only allows recovery and that final performances are related more to the type of training that precedes it than to what is done in the taper itself. It is hard to imagine how a few isolated events that occurred during a taper would be strong enough to over-ride the conditioned strength of responses developed through very extended periods of demanding training requiring specific adaptations.

> The major purpose of a taper is to allow athletes to recover from various forms of fatigue.

The most important variable for influencing competition performance is the specificity of work that precedes the taper. That work should:

- Be of the same pace as the anticipated performance level so that bio-mechanical patterns can be refined under varying levels of fatigue;
- Be of the same energy–demand ratio (aerobic : anaerobic) to that demanded in each event; and
- Require the same psychological control functions that will be needed in each race.

If a swimmer has several events, then each should be trained for specifically. A taper should continue specific-training stimuli and should eliminate all non-specific demanding training experiences. Doing other activities in taper is a waste of time and may impede recovery benefits. There is no empirical support for any form of cross-training in a taper.

Non-specific training (e.g. slow swimming, kicking, use of swimming paddles, flippers, etc.) should only be used to provide variety and low-demand recovery activities. During a taper, the body should become highly sensitized to the specific qualities required for targeted events and de-sensitized to irrelevant activities; that de-sensitization is important. When a swimmer is tired in a race, the body has to determine which established forms of activity will be recruited to assist in performance-maintenance. If there are slow-swimming patterns that are high in conditioned strength, they will be recruited and performance will suffer. If the body only knows fast-swimming patterns, then its selection options are limited to them and consequently, fast swimming will be maintained. The activities programmed in the taper should always reinforce race-specific movement patterns and energy use.

If a swimmer intends to seriously contest several races, the demands of training (and subsequently of tapering) will be more complex as the set 'paces' of all events should be trained. The difficulty with meeting this criterion is that excessive training is possible when, ideally, the training load of the taper should be reduced incrementally. To compromise this dilemma, any paces that are common to several events should be accommodated before a pace that is unique to a single event. Event preferences will also determine the importance of the selected, specific training paces in the taper phase.

> The work performed in a taper should either be race-specific quality or of a recovery nature.

A taper will allow the specific training effects that have occurred, particularly in the late specific preparatory and pre-competition training phases, to emerge. The continuing of only race-specific training will heighten an athlete's and the body's awareness of the qualities of race requirements. That heightened sensitivity will increase the consistency of competition-performance quality. An example of race-specific training is discussed in Chapter 13 of *Crowood Sports Guides: Swimming.* Broken swims are a common way of ensuring that swimmers remain 'on task' during a taper.

Research tells us that improvements in performance during taper occur without changes in VO2 max. This suggests that the primary physiological changes are likely to be associated with adaptations at the muscular level rather than with oxygen delivery. Measuring VO2 max does not adequately reflect the positive effects of tapering in swimmers. Taper does not appear to affect sub-maximal post-exercise measurements (lactate, pH, bicarbonate, base excess) and heart rate. Blood measures have not been conclusively documented as being related to the taper phenomenon and, although not measured in swimmers, muscle glycogen and oxidative mechanisms have both been observed to increase in tapers in other sports.

> Improvement in power is probably the factor most responsible for the improvement in competitive swimming performance through taper.

If it is too late to attempt to correct any physically conditioned state or bio-mechanical flaw during a taper, and it is detrimental to institute a short period of intense quality training in the belief that a 'little more' physical capability will be developed, the only option for training during a taper is specific work that yields positive affirmations of a swimmer's readiness.

Psychological factors are the major ingredients of performance that can be changed and improved during a taper. Positive thinking, self-concept, self-efficacy and performance predictions should be developed to assist in developing a healthy approach to recovery and the impending competition. Mental skills development and refinement are the major activities of tapering that will have the most direct transfer to the competitive situation. A large amount of time at training and, in particular, at the competition site, should be spent honing mental control skills; for example, practising activities such as warm-ups for specific races, focusing, controlling simulated race segments, evaluating segment goals and rehearsing mental control content. A large section of tapering content should focus on psychological skills, specific mental control rehearsals and the development of a group or team orientation.

There are a number of factors that also moderate the effects of a taper and warrant adjustments in planning:

- Young swimmers require a shorter taper period than do older swimmers. Growing children and adolescents tire and recover more quickly than do mature adults. Adjustments in taper lengths should be made according to the developmental age of each swimmer.
- With the reduced load (energy demand) associated with tapering, swimmers have to reduce their food intake. If normal eating habits and volumes are maintained, weight gains are possible, which, although minor, could have a slight detrimental effect on the swimmer.
- The first stage of a taper often produces a 'bloated' feeling because of extra water retention in the muscles. For every 1g of glycogen, 3g of water is stored. This often produces a feeling of being heavy or sluggish.
- 'Shaving down' has been shown to have mechanical and consequent physiological benefits, as well as the less tangible, psychological boost of feeling more 'sleek' in the water.
- There should be an increase in the number of high-carbohydrate meals, particularly as the competition occurs. This 'loading' should commence before travel and be maintained throughout the entire precompetition and competition period. High-carbohydrate diets assist athletes to tolerate stress.
- Athletes will usually increase their own internally-generated pressures to improve performance. The more important the competition, the greater will be the level of self-imposed pressure. Since all athletes have a limited capacity for handling pressure, it is usually wise to attempt to reduce external stresses (i.e. those that emanate from parents, officials, the media, the coach), so that total pressure is manageable.
- An important psychological theme of a taper and competition preparation should be to remove uncertainty. This can be achieved if the coach increases his/her own level of planning and communication. The better a swimmer is made aware of what will happen and how things will be organized, the less stressful will be the impending travel and competitions. If the coach changes to a noticeable elevation in preparedness and communication, a positive model will be provided for athletes of heightened preparations and better forms of conduct as the competition approaches.

If swimmers are expected to prepare better and pay attention to important details of their everyday life during a taper, the coach should model similar alterations and increases in attention to detail by planning better and communicating more frequently with swimmers.

- The main performance attribute that changes during a taper is power. Consistent measurement of power, by performing short-distance time trials, can indicate positive effects of a taper to swimmers.

- The pattern of daily activity that is established in the body, the circadian rhythm, through normal training usually does not match the timing of activities at a serious swimming meet. Circadian rhythms significantly affect the ability of an individual to perform at a particular time. Adjusting training times to better match the timing of activity that will occur at the competition, as well as time-changes that occur through travel, is something that should be programmed. When times for heats and finals are known and time adjustments made, training at those times is desirable.

> Circadian rhythms need to be synchronized with the demands of the competitive schedule for maximum performances to be achieved.

A taper period and competition-preparation phase are stressful for athletes but often more so for coaches. Heightened self-monitoring by coaches of their decisions, programmes and actions should occur. Radical alterations in behaviour can signal panic to swimmers that, in turn, could destroy their confidence and efficacy. To ensure that the coach is a constructive, rather than inappropriate, model, the following considerations should be contemplated daily:

- With regard to the type of swimming that is being performed, to what is the swimmer's body adapting? Non-specific work will have no value and can be counterproductive. Setting swims at 90 per cent intensity is meaningless to the body. The swimmer's mind may know that intention, but the body will practise only the neuromuscular patterns and stimulate the energy supply that facilitates performing at

that less than race-pace speed. Only race-specific paces that require exact energy components and stimulate competition-specific mental control will have beneficial effects on performance. Any other form of swimming should be used for recovery purposes and should not be associated with serious intentions.

> Remove all non-specific training activities, so that maladaptation will not occur.

- Are each swimmer's personal needs being accommodated? Be prepared to rest swimmers at odd times, to programme separate activities and to attend to personal requirements. The taper is too critical to persist with the convenience of group programming. The fact that it is easy for a coach to set a single programme for all swimmers to follow does not mean that it is best for all swimmers. During a taper and at competitions, coaches have to be prepared to work harder than normal, for individualized attention and programming are more demanding than singular group-control actions.

- What assessment swims have been performed to detect lazy or over-zealous swimmers? Gradual recovery, with increasingly better levels of performance, particularly in activities that require a power component, should be expected. If changes are too rapid, then a slowing of the improvement might be achieved by increasing the daily training load. If performances are poor, even though increased rest has been programmed, malingering or outside-of-swimming intrusions should be investigated. Measurement is essential for judging tapering progress. It will not affect a swimmer's potential to perform well in a race. A common means of doing this is to perform short sections of key test sets used

149

throughout the season to mark progress or race readiness, e.g. 5 × 100m or 3 × 200m, measuring times/splits/stroke rates and finishing heart rate, and so on.

• Have the swimmers been prepared to do warm-ups, recovery routines and race-simulations before travelling to the competition? A coach should not be afraid to perform event-simulations prior to important meets. If an athlete is not practised at performing between-event recovery routines prior to a competition, why should he/she be expected to be proficient at doing them under the stress of competition? There is a real programming need to perform these activities as part of normal training in the pre-competition and taper phases.

> Since swimmers are asked to alter their behaviours and become more serious as a competition approaches, the coach should model those expectations with improved planning, self-control and provision of individual attention.

The taper has traditionally been given more credit than it deserves for affecting performance. It is primarily a period that allows recovery, restitution, specific practice refinements and planning of competition behaviours. What will be exhibited in races are the beneficial effects of training prior to the taper.

The psychological activity and state of the athlete becomes increasingly more important as the taper progresses and should be the primary focus of the programme. It is incorrect to think that skills can be altered in any beneficial manner or that extra physical condition can be gained by short bouts of intense training. When a taper is started, it is too late to consider any bio-mechanical or physiological-change training. As the taper progresses, indications that performance is improving and that competition conduct activities are being practised

will have beneficial effects on the athlete's psychological state. If events are predictable, practised and accompanied by a self-efficacy of performance excellence, then a successful competition is likely. The role of the coach as the model of seriousness, control, planning and professional competence, is important for swimmers to witness if they are expected to perform in a similar manner. Positive and constructive coaching, exhibiting a capacity to cope with any problem in a competent manner, will contribute to athletes believing that all conditions exist for them to perform well.

Finally, there are some issues to be discussed in relation to the use of land training within the taper. Coaches, when questioned about land training and individualization during tapering, report that different work is done both in and out of the pool and some reduction in workloads is programmed; but is this enough? Physiotherapists involved in swimming have clear views that swimmers should stop weight-training at least six weeks before a major meet. This may help to reduce any deep-seated muscle tightness, but what about the effects of de-training? Coach Alexyev Krasikov is credited with much of the success of Russian swimming and has clear views on the integrated effects of balanced tapers. In summary, they are that dryland exercises are more easily accepted by the swimmer's body if they are administered in the following order – stretching, strength, speed, or power, and, finally, relaxation.

Coach Krasikov believes that stretching and relaxation exercises during taper help develop quickness and a relaxed, flawless swimming technique. If muscles are too tense, or swimmers cannot effectively relax them, the amplitude of movements will be severely impeded during competition, especially when swum with a fast tempo. Consecutive actions of relaxation–contraction and stretching–relaxation are very important elements of

| Exercise type | Weeks until the competiton | | | |
| --- | --- | --- | --- | --- |
| | 4 | 3 | 2 | 1 |
| 1    Coordination, flexibility, agility, reaction drills | 20min | 15min | 10min | 5min |
| 2    Maintenance of speed-endurance (Weights, VASA, swimbench, etc.) | 20min | 15min | 10min | 5min |
| 3    Relaxation techniques, stretching, etc. | 20min | 15min | 10min | 5min |
| Duration of dryland session (minutes) | 60min | 45min | 30min | 15min |
| Total dryland sessions per week | 4–5 | 4 | 3 | 1–2 |

*Fig. 130. Land training during taper.*

every movement. At the beginning of the taper, dryland has more specificity in its content, and becomes more oriented toward general maintenance during the end of the taper. Coaches and scientists seem to be at odds with each other once more. There is no empirical basis for this example, but it is undoubtedly part of a highly successful performance programme and coaching practice.

## NUTRITION

For every physical activity, the body requires energy, and the amount it needs depends on the duration and type of activity. Energy is measured in kcal and is obtained from the body stores or the food we eat. Glycogen is the main source of fuel used by the muscles for both aerobic and anaerobic exercise. If you train with low glycogen stores, you will feel constantly tired, training performance will be lower and you will be more prone to injury and illness.

A calorie (cal) is the amount of heat energy required to raise the temperature of 1g of water by 1°C from 14°C to 15°C. A kilocalorie (kcal) is the amount of heat required to raise the temperature of 1,000g of water by 1°C.

### Nutrient Balance

Carefully planned nutrition must provide an energy balance and a nutrient balance. The nutrients are:

- Proteins – essential for growth and repair of muscle and other body tissues;
- Fats – one source of energy and important in relation to fat-soluble vitamins;
- Carbohydrates – our main source of energy;
- Minerals – those inorganic elements in the body that are critical to its normal functions;
- Vitamins – water- and fat-soluble vitamins play important roles in many chemical processes in the body;
- Water – essential for normal body function and as a vehicle for carrying other nutrients. Sixty per cent of the human body is water;
- Roughage – the fibrous indigestible portion of our diet essential for a healthy digestive system.

### Nutrition for Energy

Like fuel for a car the energy we need has to be blended. The blend that competitive swimmers require is:

- 65–75 per cent carbohydrates (sugar, sweets, bread, cakes);
- 15–25 per cent fats (dairy products, oil);
- 10–15 per cent protein (eggs, milk, meat, poultry, fish).

## What Types of Fat are There?

The nature of the fat depends on the type of fatty acids that make up the triglycerides. All fats contain both saturated and unsaturated fatty acids but are usually described as 'saturated' or 'unsaturated' according to the proportion of fatty acids present. As a rough guide saturated fats are generally solid at room temperature and tend to be animal fats. Unsaturated fats are liquid at room temperature and are usually vegetable fats – there are exceptions, e.g. palm oil, a vegetable oil that contains a high percentage of saturated fatty acids.

## What Types of Carbohydrate are There?

There are two types of carbohydrate: starchy (complex) carbohydrates and simple sugars. The simple sugars are found in confectionery, muesli bars, cakes and biscuits, cereals, puddings, soft drinks and juices and jam and honey, but these food stuffs also contain fat. Starchy carbohydrates are found in potatoes, rice, bread, wholegrain cereals, semi-skimmed milk, yoghurt, fruit, vegetables, beans and pulses. Both types effectively replace muscle glycogen. The starchy carbohydrates are the ones that have all the vitamins and minerals in them as well as protein. They are also low in fat, as long as you do not slap on loads of butter and fatty sauces. The starchy foods are much more bulky, so there can be a problem in actually eating that amount of food, so supplementing with simple sugar alternatives is necessary. The digestive system converts the carbohydrates in food into glucose, a form of sugar carried in the blood and transported to cells for energy. The glucose, in turn, is broken down into carbon dioxide and water. Any glucose not used by the cells is converted into glycogen – another form of carbohydrate that is stored in the muscles and liver. However, the body's glycogen capacity is limited to about 350g (12oz); once this maximum has been reached, any excess glucose is quickly converted into fat. Base your main meal with the bulk on your plate filled with carbohydrates and small amounts of protein, such as meat, poultry and fish. The extra protein and vitamins you need will be in the starchy carbohydrates.

## Carbohydrates for Performance

Following training and competition a swimmer's glycogen stores are depleted. In order to replenish them the swimmer needs to consider the speed at which carbohydrate is converted into blood glucose and transported to the muscles. The rapid replenishment of glycogen stores is important for the swimmer who has a number of races in a meet. The rise in blood-glucose levels is indicated by a food's Glycaemic Index (GI) and the faster and higher the blood glucose rises, the higher the GI. Studies have shown that consuming high GI carbohydrates (approximately 1g/kg body wt) within 2 hours of exercise, speeds up the replenishment of glycogen stores and therefore speeds up recovery time. There are times when it is beneficial to consume lower GI carbohydrates, which are absorbed slowly over a longer period of time (2–4 hours before exercise). Eating five to six meals or snacks a day will help maximize glycogen stores and energy levels, minimize fat storage and stabilize blood glucose and insulin levels.

## Hydration

With any kind of training, and land training is certainly no different, extra attention should be given to the fluid needs of swimmers. The dictionary definition of dehydration is 'an abnormal depletion of body fluids', and it can be very damaging. The human body is 50–60 per cent water and muscle is 75 per cent water. Each cell, tissue and organ needs water to function. Therefore, it makes sense that without water, we are not going to function very well, much less than at 100 per cent of our capability.

So, how much is enough? The latest recommendation for minimum intake is to drink half your body weight in ounces of water per day. For example, if swimmer A weighs 45kg (100lb), she should drink a minimum of 50oz of water per day, which equals a little over six cups per day (one cup = 8oz). This way, water intake is more individualized instead of the standard '8 × 8oz glasses of water per day'. This amount does not include what the swimmer drinks during training! Because of the extra demands of exercise, fluids taken in during workouts are above and beyond what is needed on a regular daily basis.

We know that dehydration adversely affects the performance of an athlete. As little as a 2 per cent loss in body water (around 1kg) can affect performance anything up to 10–15 per cent. Dehydration can become serious very quickly. The table in the next column outlines the progressive effects of dehydration.

The most precise way to evaluate how much water a swimmer loses is to weigh them before and after training. This will tell you how much water was lost during one workout, and how much must be replaced. However, this is not always a good guide because the importance of this information can become muddled in translation and weight tends to become the focus instead of how much fluid was lost and should be replaced. A better way to determine hydration status is to focus on the colour of urine produced. It should be light in colour, almost clear. A dark or bright yellow colour probably means that

| Percentage Loss of Body Water | Signs of Dehydration |
|---|---|
| 0–1 | Thirst |
| 2–5 | Dry mouth, flushed skin, fatigue, headache, impaired physical performance. |
| 6 | Increased body temperature, breathing rate and pulse rate; dizziness; increased weakness. |
| 8 | Dizziness, increased weakness, laboured breathing with exercise. |
| 10 | Muscle spasms, swollen tongue, delirium. |
| 11 | Poor blood circulation, failing kidney function. |

you are not properly hydrated. Keep in mind that some multi-vitamins affect the colour of urine – usually turning it bright yellow. Do not rely on thirst to tell you if you are properly hydrated. You will not feel thirsty until you are already a little dehydrated and have lost important fluids and electrolytes.

Remember from the example that swimmer A needs to drink about 50–60oz of water every day. What about other fluids? There is no drink that swimmers have to completely avoid, but keep in mind that caffeine (and alcohol) has a dehydrating affect. It is recommend that for each soft drink, tea or coffee you drink, make up for it by drinking two extra cups of water.

The goal is to keep performance up by maintaining hydration. It is important that swimmers drink enough fluids throughout the day, but it is equally important that the coaches are setting a good example. They are in the gym/pool just as long, if not longer, than the athletes and working hard too! Coaches – you should let the swimmers see you guzzle water or some type of sports drink. Carry a water bottle with you at all times and practise what you preach!

So what's the 'scoop' on sports drinks? It was originally thought that unless you were doing strenuous exercise for 60 minutes or more, water was the best thing for you. Now there is research that supports the view that consuming sports drinks during high-intensity exercise, of 60 minutes or less, enhances aspects of performance. Sports drinks are popular for different reasons. One is that they are more palatable than water to some people; therefore the athlete ends up drinking more fluids and maintaining hydration easier. Another reason is if you have long sessions (3 hours plus), it is very important that your swimmers are re-fuelling during practice. If land training is coupled with swimming (before or after), as is often the case, a 3-hour session is not that unusual, and if swimmers have come to training immediately after school, the problem may be compounded. This can easily be solved with a quick snack or a sports drink. Drinks of 6 to 8 per cent carbohydrate are recommended because they move through the stomach into the working muscles quickest. An essential in the training bag of swimmers should be a 'spare' water bottle filled with a palatable drink and an easy to eat snack for immediate consumption after each session.

So should you encourage your swimmers to drink a sports drink in lieu of water? Hydration prior to workout is still a big consideration. It is possible that if your athlete is dehydrated when they come to the pool, a sports drink might not give them what they need as much as water would. Temperature, humidity and type of exercise play a role too. If you have a swimmer that has a hard time drinking enough water to ensure proper hydration, suggest other choices such as sports drinks, sugar-free powdered drinks or diluted juice. Of course, as the weather warms up, it is vital that you and your athletes are properly hydrated. However, hydration is something that should be enforced all year, no matter what Mother Nature is doing! Here are some quick tips to keep in mind:

- Drink at least your body weight (kg) in ounces of water per day.
- Be aware that caffeine and alcohol have a dehydrating effect.
- Drink cool fluids – this will help to cool your body, and cool fluids move through the stomach faster, thus allowing for more rapid absorption.
- Drink two to three glasses of fluid (water) about 2 hours before workout/competition – your body loses water in sweat during a good workout in an effort to keep you cool. Losses can range anywhere from one cup to two quarts an hour. Get hydrated before coming to gym!
- Drink another one to two glasses of fluid (ideally water) 5–10 minutes before start time.
- Drink every 15–20 minutes during exercise – drink early and at regular intervals.
- Drink before you get thirsty.
- After workout/competition, drink enough to quench your thirst – and then drink more!
- Monitor hydration status by the colour of your urine – it should be very pale or almost clear.

# Glossary

**1RM (one repetition maximum)** A measure of absolute strength by lifting the heaviest possible weight for one exercise. Used to calculate loadings for resistance-training sessions.

**ABCs** Agility, balance, co-ordination and speed. Part of the FUNdamentals development programme within LTAD.

**Adaptation** A principle of training relating to how the body adjusts over time to a training stimulus.

**Aerobic** Another name for endurance.

**Age Group** The division of swimmers according to age.

**ACSM** American College of Sports Medicine.

**Anaerobic** Meaning energy for exercise without oxygen.

**AIP (Asynchronous Integrated Periodization)** The organization of land- and pool-based training for maximum effect.

**Backstroke** One of the four competitive racing strokes; basically any style of swimming on your back. Backstroke is swum as the first stroke in the medley relay and second stroke in the individual medley.

**Break-Point Volume** Concept of optimizing weekly training loads.

**Breaststroke** One of the four competitive racing strokes. Breaststroke is swum as the second stroke in the medley relay and the third stroke in the individual medley.

**Butterfly** One of the four competitive racing strokes. Butterfly (nicknamed 'the fly') is swum as the third stroke in the medley relay and first stroke in the individual medley.

**Carbohydrates** The main source of food energy used by swimmers.

**Circuit Training** Also known as 'stage training', a method of organizing training in a sequential, purposeful manner.

**CKS** Catching, kicking and striking with an implement. Part of the FUNdamentals development programme within LTAD.

**Club** A registered organization within the NGB.

**Coach Education** A structured programme of development and qualifications for coaches.

**Core Stability** Term used to denote exercises to develop functional strength in stabilizing muscles throughout the body.

**Dehydration** The abnormal depletion of body fluids (water). The most common cause of cramp.

**Dryland** The exercises and conditioning programmes swimmers perform out of the water.

**DWU (Dynamic Warm-Up)** Contemporary method of preparing for resistance-training sessions.

**Flexibility** Also known as range of movement (ROM) in a joint or series of joints.

**Freestyle** One of the four competitive racing strokes. Freestyle (nicknamed 'free') is swum as the fourth stroke in the medley relay and fourth stroke in the individual medley.

**FUNdamentals** Basic movement literacy stage of LTAD.

**Hydration** The maintenance of body fluid levels.

**IM (Individual Medley)** A swimming event using all four of the competitive strokes on consecutive lengths of the race. The order must be: butterfly, backstroke, breaststroke, freestyle. Equal distances of each stroke must be swum.

**Individuality** A principle of training relating to the needs of each swimmer.

**ICAR** International Centre for Aquatic Research.

**Interval** A specific elapsed time for swimming or rest used during swim practice.

**KGBs** Kinaesthetics, gliding, buoyancy and striking with the body. Part of the FUNdamentals development programme within LTAD.

**Land Training** Another name for 'dryland'.

**LTAD (Long-Term Athlete Development)** A systematic framework for the development of swimmers from Learn to Swim to the Olympic podium.

**Long-Term Planning** A principle of training relating to the fact that performance development can taken many years.

**Macrocycle** Seasonal planning, usually over one calendar year.

**Medicine Ball** A training device available in different sizes and weights.

**Mesocycle** Element of seasonal plan, usually between six and eighteen weeks.

**Microcycle** Element of seasonal plan, usually once a week.

**NSCA** National Strength and Conditioning Association.

**NGB** National Governing Body.

**Nutrition** The sum of the processes by which a swimmer takes in and utilizes food substances.

**Overload** A principle of training relating to the amount and intensity of work.

**Periodization** The sequential organization of training.

**Plyometrics** A form of training to improve power.

**Progression** A principle of training relating to the staged improvement of fitness.

**PNF (Proprioceptive Neuromuscular Facilitation)** An effective form of flexibility training.

**Resistance Training** A form of training used to improve strength.

**Resting Heart Rate** Usually measured first thing in the morning and used to monitor fitness and health levels.

**Reversibility** A principle of training relating to the need to maintain all aspect of fitness or they will be lost (reversed) very quickly.

**RJT** Running, jumping and throwing. Part of the FUNdamentals development programme within LTAD.

**Specificity** A principle of training relating to the need to be highly precise in every aspect or training.

**Spotter** A training partner used in weight training to assist with lifting and safety.

**Stations** Separate portions of a dryland circuit.

**Stretchcords** A training device made of thick elastic or surgical tubing.

**Stretching** A training method used to improve range of motion.

**Supercompensation** The process of adaptation within the body.

**Swimbench** A training device used to replicate swimming motions on land.

**SwimSkills** A stage of LTAD.

**Swiss Ball** A training device used to improve core stability.

**Taper** The resting phase of a swimmer at the end of the season before the championship meet.

**Swimmer Pathway** The term used within British swimming to describe the entire LTAD process.

**Training Log** A training diary used to record and monitor a swimmer's training.

**Training to Compete** A stage of LTAD.

**Training to Train** A stage of LTAD.

**Variation** A principle of training relating to the blend of methods and intensities used.

**Vitamins** The building blocks of the body. Vitamins do not supply energy, but are necessary for proper health.

**Warm-Down** The recovery swimming a swimmer does after a race when pool space is available. Also known as 'swim down'.

**Warm-Up** The practice and 'loosening' up session a swimmer does before the meet or their event is swum.

**Weights** Machines, bars and plates used by swimmers performing resistance training.

# Useful Addresses

British Swimming
Harold Fern House, Derby
Square, Loughborough
LE11 5AL, UK
Tel: 01509 618700
www.britishswimming.org

English ASA
Harold Fern House, Derby
Square, Loughborough
LE11 5AL, UK
Tel: 01509 618700
www.britishswimming.org

Scottish Swimming
National Swimming Academy,
University of Stirling, Stirling
FK9 4LA, UK
Tel: 01786 466530
email:
info@scottishswimming.com
www.britishswimming.org

Irish ASA
House of Sport, Longmile
Road, Dublin 12, Eire
Tel: 00 353 1 450 1739
email:
webmaster1@swimireland.ie

Welsh ASA
Wales National Pool Swansea,
Sketty Lane, Swansea  SA2
8QG, UK
Tel: 01792 513636
email: secretary@welshasa.co.uk
www.welshasa.co.uk

IOS (Institute of Swimming)
Harold Fern House, Derby
Square, Loughborough
LE11 5AL, UK
Tel: 01509 618746

FINA (Federation
   Internationale de Natation
   Amateur)
Avenue de L'Avant – Poste 4,
1005 Lausanne, Switzerland
Tel: 41 21 310 4710
www.fina.org

BSCTA (British Swimming
   Coaches and Teachers
   Association)
Brian McGuinness,
9 Kidderminster Road,
Bromsgrove, Worcs
B61 7HL, UK
Tel: 0870 428 8424
email:enquiries@bscta.co.uk
www.bscta.com

LEN (Ligue Europeenne de
   Natation)
c/o CONI, Stadio Olympico,
Palazzina Bonifati, 00/94
Roma, Italy
Tel: 3906 3685 7870
email: lenoffice@tin.it

Australian Swimming
Swimming Australia Ltd,
Unit 12/7 Beissel Street,
Belconnen 2617, Australia
Tel: 612 6219 5600
email: swim@swimming.org.au
www.swimming.org.au

Australian Swimming Coaches
   and Teachers Association
PO Box 2175, Moorabbin,
VIC, 3189, Australia
Tel: 03 9556 5854
email: ascta.com
www.ascta.com

USA Swimming
1 Olympic Plaza, Colorado
Springs, CO 80909, USA
Tel: 719 866 4578
www.usaswimming.org

American Swimming Coaches
   Association
John Leonard, 5101 NW 21st
Ave. Suite 200, Ft. Lauderdale,
FL 33309, USA
Tel: 1-800-356-2722,
email:
asca@swimmingcoach.org
www.swimmingcoach.org

Swimming Canada
Suite 700, 2197 Riverside
Drive, Ottawa, ON, Canada,
K1H 7X3
Tel: (613) 260-1348
email natloffice@swimming.ca
www.swimming.ca

Canadian Swimming Coaches
   and Teachers Association
PO Box 1000, St. George,
ON, Canada, N0E 1N0
Tel: 519 448 4654
email: mike.finch@csca.org
csca.org/top.htm

Swimming New Zealand
Booth House Level 3,
202-206 Cuba St, Wellington,
New Zealand
Tel: 04 801 9450
email: info@swimmingnz.org.nz
www.swimmingnz.org.nz

South Africa Swimming
Johannesburg Stadium,
North Wing Ground Floor,
124 van Beek Street, New
Doornfontein, Johannesburg
094, South Africa

Tel: 27 11 404 2480
www.swimsa.co.za

National Strength and
   Conditioning Association
1885 Bob Johnson Drive,
Colorado Springs, CO 8090,
USA
Tel: +1 719-632-6722

UK Strength and Conditioning
   Association
1 Woodville Terrace, Lytham,
Lancashire FY8 5QB, UK
email: info@uksca.org.uk

British Gymnastics
Ford Hall, Lilleshall National
Sports Centre, Newport,
Shropshire TF10 9NB, UK
Tel: 0845 1297129
International: +44 1952
822300
email: information@british-
gymnastics.org
www.british-gymnastics.org

# Bibliography

ACSM (1998). 'Youth Resistance Training,' *Sports Medicine Bulletin*, Vol. 32, No2, p.28.

BBCi (2003). Interview with Zoe Baker.

Colwin, C. (1996). 'Kiphuth's Cathedral of Sweat,' *Swimming Technique* (Spring) pp. 29–30.

Costill, D. L. (1998). 'Training adaptations for optimal performance.' Invited lecture at the Biomechanics and Medicine in Swimming VIII Conference, Jyvaskulla, Finland.

Counsilman, J. E. (1968). The *Science of Swimming*, Prentice Hall (New Jersey).

Dawson, B. (1964). *The Complete Book of Dry Land Exercises for Swimming*, Pelham Books (London).

Hogg, J. M. (1972). *Land Conditioning for Competitive Swimming*. E. P. Publishing (Wakefield).

Kiphuth, R. J. H. (1950). *How to be Fit*, Nicholas Kaye (London).

Lynn, A. (2006). *Crowood Sports Guides: Swimming*, The Crowood Press.

McArthur, J (1997). *High Performance Rowing*, The Crowood Press.

Nilson, T. S., Daigneault, T., and Smith, M. (2001). *Specific Fitness Training*, FISA Coaching Manual.

Rushall, B. S. (1998). Recent Trends in Coaching Swimmers. Public Symposium, Thessaloniki, Greece.

Rushall, B. S., and Pyke, F. S. (1990). *Training for Sports and Fitness*, Macmillan Educational (Melbourne, Australia).

Rushton, C. (2003). *Swimming*, New Zealand Coaching Certification Review.

Siff, M. C. (2002). Interview with Tudor Bompa, www.t-mag.com/articles/202bompa.htm

Vornbrock, E. (1938). In Counsilman, J. E. (1977), *Competitive Swimming Manual for Coaches and Swimmers*, Bloomington (Indiana).

# Index